CONTENT

LIST OF TABLES

LIST OF FIGURES

List of Abbreviations

ADF	Augmented Dickey-Fuller
AEX	Amsterdam Exchange Index
AGARCH	Asymmetric GARCH
AIC	Akaike Information Criterion
AMEX	American Stock Exchange
AOI	All Ordinaries Index
AR	Autoregressive
ARCH	Autoregressive Conditional Heteroscedasticity
ARCH – LM	ARCH - Lagrange Multiplier
ARDL – ECM	Autoregressive Distributed Lag – Error Correction Model
ARMA	Autoregressive Moving Average
ASE	Athens Stock Exchange
ATHEX	Athens Stock Exchange Index
BDS	Brock, Dechert, and Sheinkman
BEKK – GARCH	Baba, Engle, Kraft and Kroner GARCH
BSE	Bombay Stock Exchange
CBOE	Chicago Board Options Exchange
CBOT	Chicago Board of Trade
CLRM	Classical Linear Regression Model
CME	Chicago Mercantile Exchange
CNX	Crisil National Stock Exchange Index
CRB	Commodity Research Bureau Index
CSI	China Securities Index

DAX	Deutscher Aktien Index (German Stock Index)
DF	Dickey Fuller
DJIA	Dow Jones Industrial Average
DTB	Deutsche Terminborse (German Stock Index)
EC – ARCH	Error Correction – ARCH
ECM	Error Correction Model
ECM – COC	ECM– Cost of carry
EG	Engle Granger
EGARCH	Exponential GARCH
FTSE	Financial Times Stock Exchange
GARCH	Generalised Autoregressive Conditional Heteroscedasticity
GP	Genetic Programming
HSE	Helsinki Stock Exchange
IPC	Indices de Preciosy Cotizaciones (Mexican Stock Market Index)
ISE	Istanbul Stock Exchange
J-J	Johansen-Juselius
KOSPI	Korean Composite Stock Price Index
KSE	Karachi Stock Exchange
LIFFE	London International Financial Futures Exchange
MIB	Milano Italia Borsa (Italian Stock Exchange)
MMI	Major Market Index
NASDAQ	National Association of Securities Dealers Automated Quotations
NEAT	National Exchange for Automated Trading
NSA	Nikkei Stock Average
NSE	National Stock Exchange

NYSE	New York Stock Exchange
OLS	Ordinary Least Square
RSS	Residual Sum of Squares
RRSS	Restricted Residual Sum of Squares
S&P	Standard & Poor's
SEBI	Securities Exchange Board of India
SEM	Structural Equation Modelling
SGX	Singapore Exchange
SIC	Schwartz Information Criterion
SPI	Sydney Price Index
SWARCH-L	Switching ARCH-Leverage Effect
TAIEX	Taiwan Stock Exchange (Capitalization Weighted Stock Index)
TAIFEX	Taiwan Futures Exchange
TECM	Threshold Error Correction model
TGARCH	Threshold GARCH
TYDL	Toda – Yamamoto- Dolado- Lutkepohl
UK	United Kingdom
URSS	Unrestricted Residual Sum of Squares
USA	United States of America
VAR	Vector Autoregressive
VECM	Vector Error Correction Model
VIX	Volatility Index
VLCI	Value line Composite Index

Chapter-1
Introduction

One of the important reasons for the development of derivatives worldwide is economic risk associated with trading in financial assets and commodities. In the last few decades, financial markets have undergone a tremendous change. On one hand, financial markets have been deregulated and on the other hand, financial innovation coupled with advancement in computing technology has made trading mechanism easier and automated. This has led to increased volatility in the financial markets. Fluctuations in economic variables such as interest rates have further increased risk. Management and measurement of risk have undergone a huge change. To mitigate the risk associated with the rapid fluctuations in the financial markets the demand for hedging instruments have increased. One of the most important such risk mitigation instruments is a futures contract.

A futures contract, as against a spot transaction which is an agreement to buy/sell an asset today, is an agreement to buy/sell an asset at some future date at a specified price. The person who agrees to buy/sell the asset holds a long/short position. Futures contracts are called exchange traded derivatives because they are traded on an organized exchange.

Futures contracts are standardized contracts defined by the exchange on which they are traded. In particular, the exchange defines the following:

The Underlying Asset: The underlying asset in a futures contract may be a commodity such as crude oil or a financial asset such as a stock or stock index.

The size of the contract: How much of the asset is to be delivered in one futures contract is decided by the exchange.

Delivery: For commodities, the exchange specifies the delivery procedure including the period during which delivery can be made and where delivery will be made. However, futures contracts on financial assets such as index futures are cash settled.

As a futures contract approaches its maturity or delivery date, its price converges to the price of the underlying asset in the spot market. And on the delivery date, the futures price is equal or almost equal to the spot price. The convergence of futures and spot prices is depicted in figure 1.1. The figure depicts that the difference between futures and spot prices, called basis, reduces with the passage of time and finally on the expiration of the contract basis becomes zero.

1.1 FORCE BINDING SPOT AND FUTURES PRICES—THE COST OF CARRY

The theoretical relationship between index futures prices and the prices of the underlying index is governed by the cost of carry model (Stoll and Whaley, 1990). Mathematically, the relationship can be described as follows:

$$F_t = S_t e^{(r-q)(T-t)} \dots\dots\dots\dots\dots\dots\dots\dots\dots\dots\dots\dots (1.1)$$

Where,

F_t = price of the futures contract at time t

S_t = price level of the stock index at time t

r = risk-free rate of return

q = dividend yield on the stock index

T = duration of the futures contract so that (T − t) is time to maturity

Figure 1.1: Convergence of Futures and Spot Prices-

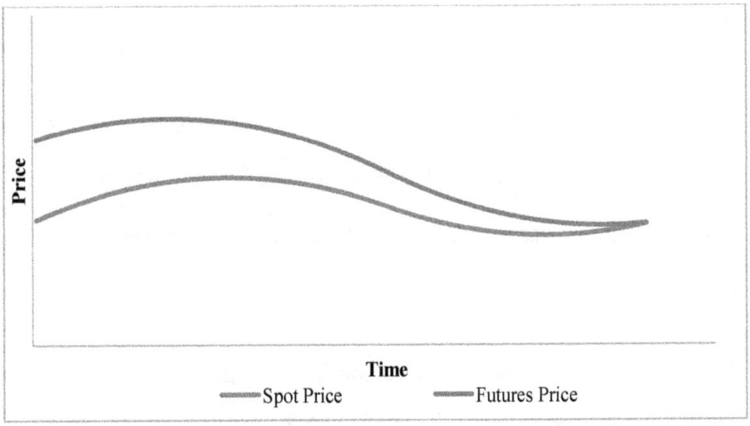

Source: Compiled by Author

The above cost of carry model summarizes the relationship between the prices of a futures contract and the underlying index. The model holds if dividend yield and risk-free rate of return are known and non-stochastic. The force binding the futures and spot prices together is 'arbitrage'. If the futures price is higher than what is implied by the cost of carry above, then risk-free profit can be earned by buying the stocks making up the index and selling the associated futures contract. On the contrary, if the futures price is less than what is implied by the cost of carry, then risk-free profit can be earned by buying the futures contract and selling the stocks comprising the index.

1.2 PRICE DISCOVERY AND LEAD-LAG RELATIONSHIP BETWEEN SPOT AND FUTURES MARKETS-

Spot and futures markets deal in the same asset traded at different points in time. Because the same asset is traded in the spot and futures markets, there should be some kind of a co-movement in the prices in these two markets. Therefore, these spot and futures markets should react to the new information in similar ways. It implies that the price in the spot market of an asset must move in unison with the price of its associated futures contract in the derivatives market; otherwise arbitrage opportunities would exist.

However, when price changes in one market are followed by price changes in another market, then a lead-lag relationship exists. The market in which price changes occur first is called the leading market and the market which follows is called lagging market.

When it is said that market i leads market j, it implies that market i is more informationally efficient. It can also be stated that price discovery takes place in market i which implies that new information is first impounded into the prices of market i and subsequently transmits to market j.

Variables which have a strong co-movement and are bound by some force which does not allow them to drift apart too far away are said to be cointegrated. In the short run, cointegrated variables may deviate from their relationship, but in the long-term, they are bound to return to the equilibrium relationship. Spot and futures prices are bound by cost of carry relationship. If spot and futures price series could drift apart without any bound, then arbitrage opportunities would exist.

According to Stoll and Whaley (1990), infrequent trading of the component stocks of the index and presence of transactions cost are some of the reasons for violation of the cost of carry relationship. Bhatia (2007) has reviewed extensively the reasons for the lead-lag relationship between futures and spot markets. Market with lower transaction costs, greater liquidity and lesser restrictions is likely to process information with greater speed and accuracy, thereby playing a more important role in price discovery. Viewed from this perspective, futures market is more likely to assimilate new information because it has lower transaction costs, in-built leverage and fewer restrictions. However, changes in the spot prices constitute part of the information set used by traders in the futures market, therefore, spot market may also lead futures market.

1.3 NEED AND PURPOSE OF THE STUDY

Understanding the relationship between futures and spot markets is of paramount importance for hedgers, speculators and arbitrageurs alike. Especially, the characteristics of returns and volatility of financial markets have implications for regulators and portfolio managers. The dynamic relationship between futures and spot markets helps to understand the information transmission mechanism.

CNX Nifty is the most recognized barometer of stock market activity in India. CNX Nifty futures allow portfolio managers and hedgers to economically execute trading strategies based on Nifty. Therefore, it is important to investigate the informational role of the futures and spot market. More specifically, there is a need to study the intraday price discovery and volatility spillovers between the markets. Understanding information transmission mechanism may enable investors to more successfully implement Nifty trading strategies. In other words, Investors can formulate better trading strategies if they have better understanding of the information transmission mechanism.

The present study is an attempt to investigate the temporal relationship between futures market and the underlying spot market in India. Although considerable attention has been given to examine the relationship between stock index and stock index futures, only a few studies have examined the relationship between individual stock and stock futures.

This study investigates the empirical intraday returns and volatility relationship between CNX Nifty Futures and its underlying Index as well as relationship between returns and volatility of individual stocks that constitute CNX Nifty.

The present study is different from prior studies in several ways. Firstly, the study has considered individual stocks along with stock index for investigating the temporal relationship. Secondly, the study has utilized high frequency (5-min) data which is of paramount importance these days. Finally, the study has also examined the second moment linkages, i.e., volatility relationship between the two markets.

The present study is an attempt to characterize empirically the dynamic interactions and interdependence of the stock market and the futures market returns. The primary objective is to find out whether futures price changes provide predictive information regarding spot price changes and/or vice versa. Specifically, the study addresses the following questions:

Is there any equilibrium relationship between the spot and futures markets? Specifically, Are the spot and futures markets cointegrated?

Is there any lead-lag relationship between the two markets? Specifically, are past returns of one market helpful in predicting future returns in the other market?

Are the two markets interlinked through their second moments? Specifically, does volatility in each market spillover to the other market?

Do good and bad news influence the markets in a different way? Specifically, are there any asymmetric influences exerted by each market on the volatility of another market?

To answer these questions, the study employs a number of tools & techniques of time series econometrics.

1.4 CHAPTER SCHEME

The thesis is divided into six chapters. A brief outline of each of the chapters is given below:

Chapter 1 (Introduction) introduces the study. It describes the basic relationship between futures and spot markets and presents the need and purpose of the study.

Chapter 2 (Review of Literature) describes and extensive survey of previous researches relevant for the study.

Chapter 3 (Research Methodology) lists the objectives and hypotheses. It also discusses in detail data used and methodology employed.

Chapter 4 (Empirical Evidence on Returns Relationship between Futures and Spot Markets) analyzes the returns relationship between futures and spot markets for CNX Nifty and all its fifty constituent stocks.

Chapter 5 (Empirical Evidence on Volatility Spillover between Futures and Spot Markets) presents empirical evidence regarding volatility linkages between the two markets for the index and individual stocks.

Chapter 6 *(Findings and Conclusion)* summarizes the study and discusses findings and conclusion. It also lists the limitations of the study and suggests areas for future research.

Chapter -2
Review of Literature

Hedgers, arbitrageurs, speculators, regulators, policy makers, portfolio managers and academicians are interested in understanding futures and spot market relation for obvious reasons. Therefore, relationship between spot and futures markets has been a matter of vast theoretical and empirical research. Across the globe, researches have been conducted by employing varied methodologies and using data at different frequencies. This chapter reviews relevant existing literature on price discovery, lead-lag relationship and volatility linkages between futures and spot markets. The literature reviewed in the present study is grouped into the following two broad categories:

- Studies on relationship in the first moment, i.e., returns relationship

- Studies on relationship in the second moment, i.e., volatility relationship

The remainder of the chapter is organised as follows. Section 2.1 covers the research studies pertaining to price discovery and lead-lag relationship for returns between spot and futures markets. Section 2.2 presents the studies on volatility spillover between the two markets; and, section 2.3 concludes with the research gap.

Based on the main objectives of the study, the literature reviewed is grouped into two categories as follows:

2.1   Studies on lead-lag relationship for returns between spot and futures markets.

2.2   Studies on volatility spillovers between spot and futures markets.

2.1 STUDIES ON LEAD-LAG RELATIONSHIP FOR RETURNS BETWEEN SPOT AND FUTURES MARKETS

Cox (1976) examined how the information in spot market is affected by organized futures trading. He suggested two reasons for futures market being informative for spot market. First, futures markets may attract speculators, and second, futures markets have lower transactions costs. For studying the effect of futures trading, Cox developed a model of spot-price behaviour and market information. Analysing the data for six commodities, he concluded that existence of futures trading seems to make the working of the spot market more efficient.

According to **Brannen and Ulveling (1984),** futures market would develop for information exchange if the current spot prices are noisy and hence fail to convey all information. They studied how the existence of futures trading alters information and price expectations differences among traders. Analysing data from the commodities markets, they found that price differences among traders reduce with the addition of the futures price.

Kawaller, Koch, and Koch (1987) used high frequency minute-to-minute data for all the transaction days during 1984 and 1985 to examine price relationship between S&P 500 index and the associated futures contracts. They studied the price discovery role of futures market and also investigated price relationship on and around expiration day. Using three stage least squares, they concluded that futures market consistently leads spot market by twenty to forty five minutes and spot market very infrequently leads futures market by not more than one minute. Their study did not find any substantially different contemporaneous price relationship on the expiration day than on non-expiration days.

Using Granger Causality test, **Ng (1987)** examined the informational efficiency of futures market for a variety of financial assets including S&P 500 and the Value Line Composite Index. Ng suggested some of the reasons why a lead-lag may exist between futures and spot markets. Transaction cost and short-selling restrictions have been suggested as some of the reasons which may cause futures market to lead the spot market. Using daily data for the time period from April 21, 1982 to December 31, 1986 for S&P 500 index, Ng, on the basis of the rejection of the null hypothesis that futures market does not granger cause spot market, concluded that new information is first reflected in the futures market. Similar conclusion is drawn regarding the Value Line Composite Index.

Laatsch and Schwarz (1988) investigated the relative price discovery roles of Major Market Index and MMI futures by employing both daily and minute-by-minute data from July 24, 1984 until September 19, 1986. They used a partial equilibrium model suggested by Garbade and Silber (1983). The study found that during the market evolution phase the pattern of lead-lag relationship between spot and futures markets was fluctuating. However, as the futures market evolved, MMI futures largely perform the role of price discovery. Further, they concluded this leadership of futures market is due to variables other than non-synchronous trading of the component stocks in the index.

Stoll and Whaley (1990) studied the temporal relation between S&P 500 and Major Market Index in a multiple regression framework. They used 5-min data from April 1982 until March 1987. First, they examined in detail the time series characteristics of intraday returns in spot and futures markets for both the indices. They developed a model for describing the effects of bid-ask spreads and infrequent trading of component stocks and used ARMA type models for removing these effects. Even after controlling for the effects of the infrequent trading and bid-ask spreads, they reported that futures market lead spot market by about five to ten minutes. However, spot market was also found to have mild predictive power to affect futures market.

Chan (1992) made an investigation whether MMI futures and S&P 500 futures contracts lead/lag MM cash index and the underlying stocks. Using 5-min data for the time periods (August 1984 through June 1985 and from January 1987 through September 1987) in the framework of a multiple regression model, they provided evidence that lead-lag relations exist between MM cash index and the futures contracts (MMI futures as well as S&P 500 futures). However, lead from futures to spot market was much stronger than from cash to futures. In addition, the leading role of the futures market was reported to be stronger in the presence of market wide information.

Wahab and Lashgari (1993) employed cointegration analysis to investigate the causal relations between stock index and associated futures contracts for S&P 500 and FTSE 100 indexes. Using daily closing prices data over the period from 1988 to 1992, they reported a feedback relationship between spot and futures markets for both the indexes. However, they found that spot market played a stronger leading role.

Ghosh (1993) investigated whether spot and futures price changes are forecastable. He employed intraday data for S&P 500 index and daily data for CRB index. The result supported the existence of stable long term relationship between the spot and futures markets. The study found that the direction of flow of information is from futures to spot in case of S&P 500 index and from spot to futures in CRB index.

Abhyankar (1995) used hourly data from 1986 through 1990 to examine the lead-lag relationship between FT-SE 100 stock index and the associated futures index under varying market conditions. Using a multiple regression approach, he found that futures market leads the underlying index under varying phases of trading activity and during periods of high conditional volatility. He further reported that during periods of moderate (normal) news, the futures market is found to lead; during good news, no market is found to lead/lag; and during periods of bad news, no discernible pattern of lead/lag exists.

Hung and Zhang (1995) analysed the long-run equilibrium relationship between the Municipal Bond Index (MBI) and its futures contract by using Cointegration analysis and short-run dynamics and price movements in both the markets by using Error Correction Model. The results suggest that price movements are contemporaneous and there is a two way feedback system between the markets. By splitting the sample period from June, 1985 to April 1993 into two sub periods, it was reported that spot market serves a major role in making adjustment towards the long-run equilibrium relationship in the first sub-sample period. On the other hand, in the second sub-sample period futures market plays greater role in restoring long-run equilibrium.

Tse (1995) had taken Nikkei Stock Average (NSA) futures and spot index traded in Japanese stock market data from December 1988 through January 1993, to determine the lead-lag relationship between them. He analysed daily data by using two version of Error Correction Model depending upon the postulated long-run relationship between markets. The findings are indicative of price discovery function of futures market. Further, univariate time series model and VAR model were also employed in the study but the performance of the Error Correction Model was found to be superior.

Hasbrouck (1995) suggested an information share based econometric approach for measuring the price discovery role of markets. He applied this technique to measure the price discovery for stocks traded on NYSE and the regional stock exchanges. He stated that the random walk component of a security's price can be viewed as its implicit efficient price. Hasbrouck defined the information share as the proportion of the variance of the efficient price innovation attributed to a market which in turn is a measure of a market's contribution to price discovery. His study concluded that the price discovery role is largely performed by NYSE.

Fleming, Ostdiek and Whaley (1996) tested the trading cost hypotheses by analysing the temporal relationships among returns of S&P 500 futures, S&P 100 options and there underlying stock index portfolios. Using 5 minute return data they evidenced that S&P 500 index futures and S&P 100 index options were leading the underlying spot market index in terms of returns. Besides, S&P 500 futures were also found to lead the S&P 100 option index, supporting the trading cost hypotheses. Their study concluded that price discovery takes place in index derivatives market where trading costs are considerably lower than the stock market. However, for individual stocks price discovery takes place in the stock market because of lower trading cost than option market.

By using daily data, **Huang, Masulis and Stoll (1996)** examined relationship between returns of oil futures and U.S. stock returns. They analysed the repercussions of energy shocks from the perspective of financial markets. Utilizing vector autoregressive (VAR) approach, they found that oil futures returns are uncorrelated with stock market returns. They further reported that oil futures returns significantly lead oil stocks returns by one day. However, they added that such lead has small economic significance.

Fortenbery and Zapata (1997) made an attempt to study the price discovery and long-term relationship between Cheddar Cheese cash and futures market. Their study found no evidence of presence of stable long-term pricing relationship between the markets. Besides, neither of the markets was found to lead the other in price discovery process.

Chathrath and Song (1998) studied the intraday behaviour of Japanese yen spot and futures rates (traded on CME), around a sets of 20 macroeconomic announcements over the period from January 1992 through December, 1995. Their study provided evidence regarding futures rate leading the spot rate of Japanese yen and making spot market volatile. They concluded that futures markets' are reacting more efficiently to new information.

Pizzi, Economopoulos and O' Neill (1998) attempted to investigate the price discovery process in the S&P 500 cash index and its 3-month and 6-month futures contracts. By using minute-by-minute data for the period January, 1987 through March, 1987, they found significant cointegration among futures index (both 3-month and 6-month) and cash index, indicating existence of long-term equilibrium. The result of their study revealed that both the three and six month futures market of S&P

500 index lead the spot market by at least 20 minutes. Besides, they also reported that spot market very infrequently leads the futures market by three to four minutes.

Jong and Donders (1998) tested the intraday lead-lag relationship between derivatives and cash market by dividing the sample period into two sub-periods. They concluded that futures market leads both option and underlying cash market of AEX Index by five to ten minutes on an average.

Abhyankar (1998) used 5-min intraday data for FT-SE index and for four FT-SE futures contracts expiring in 1992 for the months of March, June, September and December. Using raw, ARMA filtered, and EGARCH filtered returns in the framework of a linear causal test, he reported that futures market leads the cash market by about 5 to 15 minutes. However, using a nonlinear causality test based on Baek and Brock approach, the study found bidirectional causal relationship between futures and spot markets.

Booth, So and Tse (1999) in their article empirically examined the price discovery process among stock, futures and options indices of DAX securities traded on FSE in Germany. They showed that the FDAX and DAX respond to new information faster than ODAX. They further observed that because FDAX supports transaction costs hypothesis, they contribute more to price discovery as compared to ODAX.

Cohen (1999) tested two hypotheses, first, whether derivatives leads to excess volatility in the cash market, and second, whether they facilitate price discovery. Using bond and equity indices of US, Japan and Germany, they concluded that there is no clear evidence that derivatives destabilizes the spot market and makes price discovery more stable.

Min and Najund (1999) examined the lead-lag relationship between KOSPI 200 and associated futures index in Korea. Using 10-min intraday data from May 3, 1996 through October 16, 1996 in the framework of three stage least squares, they reported that returns in the futures market lead spot market returns by about 30 minutes.

Silvapulle and Moosa (1999) investigated causal relationship between spot and futures prices of WTI crude oil during the period between 2 January, 1985 and 11 July, 1996. The study showed that both markets react to new information simultaneously and there exists bidirectional non-linear causality between the markets. Using linear causality test they found that daily futures prices lead spot prices, but the leading pattern of futures changes over time.

Using Hasbrouck (1995) cointegration model, **Tse (1999)** found that in intraday price discovery DJIA futures dominates cash market. For this purpose, he used minute-by-minute cash and futures prices data for DJIA for the period from November 1997 to April 1998.

Kim, Szakmary and Schwarz (1999) attempted to study the trading cost hypothesis that market with lower trading cost will react more quickly to new information. They used intraday data of S&P 500, NYSE Composite and MMI futures indices and their respective cash indices for the period from January, 1986 to July, 1991. They focused on the intraday price leadership across these futures indices and their respective cash indices, rather than between each spot and its associated futures index. They found that among the futures indices S&P 500 leads the other two (NYSE composite and MMI) by five minutes because of its lower trading cost. They further reported that in cash market indices leadership role is played by the MMI cash index, following the proposition of trading cost hypothesis. In short, their study revealed that market with lower trading cost plays the price discovery role.

In the Australian markets, **Frino, Walter and West (2000)** empirically examined the lead-lag relationship between SPI futures contracts (futures index) and All Ordinaries Index (spot index) around information release. Using minute-by-minute data for the period from August 1, 1995 to December 31, 1996, they found that the leading role of stock index futures over spot index strengthens around the release of macro-economic information and weakens around firm specific information. Besides, feedback from spot to futures is found to strengthen around the release of stock specific information.

Brooks, Rew and Ritson (2001) used 10-min intraday data and found that for FTSE 100 index, futures returns lead the cash returns. They compared various forecasting models for finding if any profitable trading can be made. They concluded that the best model is the error correction model.

Chan and Lien (2001) examined the impact of cash settlements on the ability of futures market to predict futures prices. They took two commodities- Feeder cattle and live/lean Hog futures, on which futures contracts are available. By adopting Geweke feedback measure, they found that cash settlements of contracts improve the price discovery function of Feeder cattle futures contracts and the two markets become integrated. They further concluded that replacement of physical delivery by cash settlement makes the price discovery function of lean hog futures contracts less effective as before.

Thenmozhi (2002) examined the effect of futures trading S&P CNX Nifty futures traded on National stock Exchange of India. She found that futures trading transmits information to spot market and futures market is also faster in processing information and leads spot market by one day.

Using 5-min data from January, 1999 to June, 1999, **Roope and Zurbruegg (2002)** compared the informational efficiency of Taiwan Futures Exchange and Singapore Exchange for the Taiwan Futures contracts listed in the two exchanges. Employing the Hasbrouck (1995) and Gonzalo-Granger (1995) information content based methodologies, they reported that futures markets dominate price discovery over spot markets and Singapore futures market over Taiwan futures market.

Sahadevan (2002) analysed data of six commodities futures, traded on four Exchanges and found that these exchanges fail to provide efficient hedge against the risk emerging from the volatility of prices of commodities. In other words, the results of the study indicated that futures market of these commodities is not efficient. He also reported that both futures and spot markets are not integrated.

Beaulieu, Ebraham and Morgan (2003) investigated the price discovery role of the futures contract and exchange-traded fund available for the same market index by dividing the sample period into two sub- periods. Their findings are indicative of the role of futures that remains the same, i.e. leading in price discovery in both sub periods, as compared to ETFs. They argued that the possible reason behind this may be small tick size.

Lien and Yang (2003) employed the Geweke measure of information flow to examine whether the price discovery function increased after the cash settlement was replaced by physical delivery in case of futures contracts on individual shares in Australia. For cash settlement as well as for physical delivery, their study found a significant flow of information from spot to futures market. They added that this role of spot was further enhanced after switching from cash settlement to physical delivery of the futures contracts. Thus, they ended up finding domination of spot market over futures in price discovery process.

Raju and Karande (2003) studied the price discovery and volatility effect of Nifty futures on Nifty spot index traded on NSE of India. Analysis of daily closing values on Nifty Index revealed that price discovery takes place in both the markets.

Adopting a non-parametric Genetic Programming (GP) approach for identifying structural changes for examining lead-lag relationship between daily returns on Nikkei 225 spot and futures indices, **Lien, Tse and Zhang (2003)** concluded that spot market play a dominant role in price discovery during extreme periods. They also employed linear Granger Causality test and reported leading role of futures market.

Covrig, Ding and Low (2004) studied how Singapore Exchange, a small satellite market contributes to price discovery. They also attempted to explain the possible reasons behind this. For this purpose they took Nikkei 225 index traded on three different markets, viz., TSE, OES and SGX. These three markets are informationally linked and compete for trade flow. The methodology employed includes the information share based approach of Hasbrouck (1995) and the common factor component method of Gonzalo and Granger (1995). They found that the overall futures market contributes 77% to price discovery. They stated that contribution to price discovery of satellite market lies in its careful design of contract details and trading mechanisms.

Zhong, Darrat and Otero (2004) investigated the price discovery process between IPC index and associated futures contracts in Mexico. Using daily data from April 15, 1999 to July 24, 2002 in the context of bivariate error-correction EGARCH (EC-

EGARCH), they concluded that price discovery function is largely performed by the futures market.

So and Tse (2004) studied the information transmission mechanism for the Hang Seng index (HIS), the Hang Seng futures index and the tracker fund. Using minute-to-minute data from November 12, 1999 through June 28, 2002 in the framework of information share based approaches of Hasbrouck (1995), and Gonzalo and Granger (1995), they found that futures market dominates price discovery followed by spot market. They also reported that Tracker fund contributes little in the matter of price discovery.

Sah and Omkarnath (2005) found that futures rate is not a predictor of spot rate. Taking the daily values of near month contract of S&P CNX Nifty futures traded on NSE for the period from 12 June, 2000 to 29 January, 2004, they concluded that futures market is not efficient.

Tse, Bandyopadhyay and Shen (2006) explored the price discovery role of futures between the DJIA index and three futures contracts available on this index- the DAIMOND exchange traded fund, the DJIA futures and the electronically traded mini-futures. The authors also used S&P 500 index (ETF and futures) to do duplicate analysis for checking the robustness of the result. They found that ETF derivatives dominate over ETF shares for price discovery function. Their results remained robust when the analysis was performed using the S&P 500 regular futures, and the E-mini futures. Among the three futures contracts, Mini-futures were found to dominate others in price discovery role and contributed about 69.1%. Whereas ETF and S&P 500 futures contributed 28.6% and 49% respectively in price discovery function.

Using daily data for CNX Nifty, **Gupta and Singh (2006)** examined the price discovery role of the futures market. Their study provided evidence in support of the hypothesis that futures market in India serves as a price discovery vehicle.

Gupta and Singh (2006) determined the weak form efficiency of Indian futures market by taking Nifty futures index and 24 stock futures available on NSE. They found that at index level no lead-lag relationship exists whereas at the level of individual stocks, futures market leads spot market.

Mukherjee and Mishra (2006) used 1-min intraday data from April to September 2004 for investigating lead-lag relationship between CNX Nifty and associated futures index as well as between the spot and futures markets of five individual stocks. By employing a multiple regression approach, they found that feedback relationship exists between CNX Nifty and CNX Nifty futures, however, CNX Nifty plays a dominant role in the matter of price discovery. For the five individual stocks also, they found a feedback relationship with spot market playing a dominant role.

Praveen and Sudhakar (2006) in their study empirically investigated the price discovery mechanism of India's Commodity futures market. By taking the daily figures of Nifty futures traded on NSE and Gold futures traded on MCX of India for the period of April, 2002 to June, 2005, they tried to compare the commodity futures market with mature equity futures market available on NSE. Their results support the presence of mature stock markets which facilitates the price discovery function at NSE. Contrary to this, the commodities futures market is less mature making itself a platform of price discovery process by assimilation of market flow of information. The reason behind this may be that spot gold in India is not confined to one place like single futures market available at NSE for equity futures.

Mukherjee and Mishra (2006) used the daily data of Nifty index and some selected Nifty stocks for the period from June 2000 to September 2004, to find out how the co-movements of price in both spot as well as derivatives market depends upon flow of information in these markets and how it varies with time. They applied 'Geweke Measure of Feedback' to both index as well individual stocks of Nifty. The results confirmed that there is a significant flow of information from spot to futures at index level of CNX Nifty and there is instantaneous flow of information between spot and futures market. At the stock level, except for 8 stocks, all the other stocks futures were found to be leading spot during the whole study period. In short, the results provide mixed evidence on the lead-lag relationship which is dynamic and stock specific.

Kakati and Kakati (2006) examined the informational content of the basis and price discovery role of the Indian futures market. They found that there is bidirectional flow of information between spot and futures market followed by a moderate feedback system when long lags are taken. They also found the informational role of basis in predicting the direction of change in futures prices and also spot prices but to a lesser extent.

Sah and Kumar (2006) employed Engle-Granger ECM and Cointegration model to test the price discovery of Indian futures market over spot market. The findings support the leading role of futures and provide evidence that there exists a feedback mechanism between Nifty spot and futures.

Pradhan and Bhat (2006) studied the price discovery and causal relation between the futures and spot market of Nifty Index, by using near-month, mid-month and far-month contracts and employing J-J Cointegration and VECM model. Their analysis established the leading role of underlying cash market in information transmission and price discovery.

Gupta and Singh (2006) investigated the hypothesis whether Indian futures market serves as an efficient price discovery vehicle for the spot market. They found the leading role of futures with bilateral causality.

Brandt, Kavajech and Underwood (2007) undertook regression analysis to investigate whether price discovery takes place in US treasury cash and futures market and how environmental forces impact the information flow from one market to another. Utilizing both market prices and net orderflow it was observed that the direction and magnitude of price discovery in the two markets is influenced by environmental variables considered in the study. They reported that although price discovery takes place in futures market but the presence of illiquidity due to wide bid-ask spreads in the cash market is the reason for more price discovery in the cash market as asymmetric information is high.

Bose (2007) made her contribution by investigating whether stock index futures market plays an important role in the assimilation of information and price discovery process by taking the futures prices data of Nifty Index traded on NSE. She found that significant information flows from futures to spot over the period of four years and seven months indicating that the prices/returns of futures are more informative than that of spot.

Using 5-min data from April to March 2006 and employing error correction model, **Bhatia (2007)** found that price discovery takes place in both the futures and the spot markets. However, futures market is found to be more efficient and leads the spot market by 10 to 25 minutes.

Gupta and Singh (2007) investigated the arbitrage efficiency of futures market in India. Using data from June, 2000 to December, 2005, they found presence of long-run (equilibrium) relationship between the two markets. In addition, they reported bilateral flow of information, indicating that neither of the markets was leading each other.

Anand (2007) examined the efficiency of Indian Commodities Futures Market by studying 12 commodities traded on NCDEX for contracts expiring on May 2006. The results showed that only Gur and Gold have achieved market efficiency to recognizable extent while the other commodities exhibited this relationship with a considerable lag and in some cases, with a bilateral causality or reverse causality.

Using a non-parametric approach, **Illueca and Lafuente (2008)** analyzed the destabilizing effect of mini-futures trading in Spanish stock market on the distribution of returns in the spot market and to test their contribution in the process of price discovery. By estimating the conditional densities of the returns in spot market under varying levels of trading volume in mini futures of IBEX index, they tested effect of mini futures trading on the distribution of spot returns. Empirical evidence suggested that trading of mini futures does not destabilize the spot market as the spot returns do not depend on the expected trading in mini futures.

Further, results also revealed that with the introduction of mini-futures price discovery enhanced.

Kavussanos, Visvikis and Alexakis (2008) employed daily data from February, 2000 to June, 2003 to examine the informational efficiency of two futures indexes viz., FTSE/ATHEX-20 and FTSE/ATHEX Mid-40 contracts in Greece. They reported bidirectional linkages between futures and cash markets, however, the lead from futures to cash is found to be much stronger than in the reverse direction.

Shastri, Thirumalai and Zutter (2008) found the price discovery role of 137 Single Stock Futures traded on OneChicago exchange. The results of their study supported the price discovery function of SSFs market. It was also reported in the study that SSFs trading improved the quality of underlying stocks.

Fung and Tse (2008) used intraday data of bid-ask quotes of the Hong-Kong Single-Stock futures (SSFs) contracts and their underlying stocks over the period from August, 2001 to June, 2003, to investigate their operational and pricing efficiency. They concluded that the futures market is informationally efficient and futures quotes provides for one-third of price discovery despite of their low volume because they were fairly priced.

Kang and Park (2008) in their article focused on the liquidity and the information effects in market dynamics of returns and order imbalances across stock, futures and options of KOSPI index securities. Their evidences suggest that information effect is more pronounced than the liquidity effect and returns are more predictive of futures prices than order imbalances. In short, they found that derivatives market generally leads their underlying spot market because informed traders prefer to trade in these derivatives contracts.

Mallikarjunappa and Afsal E M (2008) used 1-min data for 12 stocks traded on NSE for studying lead-lag relationship between futures and spot markets in India. Using VECM-EGARCH specification, they found feedback relationship between the two markets.

Bose (2008) studied the characteristics of the Indian Commodity futures market, in order to determine whether these markets were having the same features as present in the equity futures market. The study used spot and futures prices data of multi-commodity and agricultural commodities indices. It was found that in terms of informational efficiency multi-commodity indices behave similar to equity indices. She concluded that futures market can serve as an effective hedging instrument for commodities.

Reddy and Sebastin (2008) employed the entropic analysis approach for studying the temporal relationship between spot and futures markets in India. For this purpose, they used data over the period of October, 2005 to September, 2006. They concluded that information dissemination first takes place in futures market and then it is transmitted to spot market.

Debasish and Mishra (2008) used hourly data from July, 2001 through March, 2007 for studying lead-lag relationship between spot and derivatives markets for CNX Nifty. Using multiple regression approach, they found that futures market leads spot market.

Cabrera, Wang and Yang (2009) studied the three foreign exchange markets – the CME GLOBEX regular futures, E-mini futures and the EBS (electronic Broking Services) interdealer spot market, to investigated the price discovery of Euro and Japanese Yen Exchange Rates. They found evidence of spot leading the futures market. Foreign exchange spot prices are found to be more informative than the regular futures and mini-futures markets, thus for both the exchange rates (Euro and Japanese Yen) spot market leads the futures in price discovery process.

Li (2009) combined markov switching process with vector error correction model for studying the dynamic relationship between spot and futures markets under high-low volatility regimes. For this purpose, he examined three mature markets namely, USA (S&P 500), UK (FT-SE 100), Germany (DAX 30) and two emerging markets namely, Brazil (Bovespa) and Hungry (BSI). Using daily data from April, 1995 through December, 2005, the study reported that during low variance state price discovery takes place in the futures markets, however, during volatile periods (high variance state), spot markets serve the role of price discovery.

Schlusche (2009) used the German DAX ETF, Futures and spot to determine the price discovery role of futures market. The analysis showed clear price leadership of futures over both spot and ETF. They contented that volatility is the main force behind price discovery as conjectured by trading cost hypothesis. They also found that in periods of low to high volatility, price formation decreases in the futures market.

Using daily data for CNX Nifty futures and the underlying index, **Karmakar (2009)**, on the basis of a Vector Error Correction Model (VECM), concluded that price discovery function is performed by futures market.

Pati and Padhan (2009) examined lead-lag and causal relationship between CNX Nifty and CNX Nifty futures by using VECM and Toda-Yamanoto-Dolado-Lutkepohl (TYDL) causality test. Using daily data from January 2004 to December 2008, they found that there is uni-directional causality from futures to spot market. They also used impulse response and variance decomposition and reported that futures market leads the spot market.

Srinivasan (2009) examined the relation between commodities derivatives and the underlying assets for nine selected Oil and Gas industry stocks in India. Using daily data series from May 12, 2005 to January 29, 2009, he found that there exists a long-run relationship between spot and futures price of these commodities. Out of nine stocks of oil industry, four are found to have bidirectional relationship, three stocks have unidirectional relationship from spot to futures and rest two have unidirectional relationship from futures to spot.

Using 1-min data from 2004 to 2007, **Gupta and Singh (2009)** investigated the price discovery and lead-lag relationship between futures and spot markets in India. They carried out the analysis for CNX Nifty index as well as for fifty actively traded stocks. They used Granger Causality test and reported that Nifty futures leads Nifty by five minutes. Further, they found that individual stocks lead/lag in the range of five to fifty five minutes. They concluded that price discovery takes place in both the markets with futures market playing a larger role.

Wats and Mishra (2009) found that both the spot and futures markets aid each other in determining the price in the other market, however, significant role is played by the futures market. These findings are in conformity with other studies undertaken in Indian markets.

Reddy and Sebastain (2009) used the entropy analysis approach to examine the dynamic relationship between spot and futures markets for commodities as well as equities. They found that there exists feedback relationship between the two markets and past information for up to 6 days is relevant.

Srinivasan (2009) found that both spot and futures markets of S&P CNX Nifty index observes a stable long run relationship. He also concluded that there exists bidirectional causality and both the markets are informationally efficient. Thus, the study provides evidence that both the markets contributes to price discovery.

Shakeel (2009) used daily data for studying price discovery and lead-lag relationship between CNX Nifty and its futures index. Using cointegration analysis and Granger Causality, he found that it is the spot market which leads the futures market.

Using intraday data at the frequency of 3-min from March 5, 2004 through July 1, 2004 in the framework of a Threshold Regression Model (TRM), **Tse and Chan (2010)** examined the lead-lag relationship between S&P 500 and associated futures index. They found that lead from S&P 500 to S&P 500 futures diminishes due to presence of short selling restrictions in the spot market. Consistent with previous researches, they reported that in the presence of market wide information futures market play a stronger leading role over the spot market. In addition, their study also found that during periods of directionless trading, spot market exhibits stronger leading effect over futures market.

Chang (2011) examined the informational content of basis (spot price minus futures price) for studying the price discovery function of SGX CNX Nifty futures traded on Singapore Stock Exchange. He found stronger/weaker role of futures market in terms of strengthening negative/positive basis under negative prior shocks.

Using 5-min data from March 1, 2007 through January 31, 2008, **Pati and Rajib (2011)** investigated the relationship between Nifty futures and the underlying spot index. On the basis of Granger Causality test, they concluded that uni-directional causality runs from futures to spot market.

Jackline and Deo (2011) studied the intertemporal relationship in Indian Stock Market between cash and derivative segments. They concluded by using VECM model that for CNX Nifty cash market plays a leading role over the futures market.

Debasish (2011) reported the directional causality in spot and futures market of six leading sectors by taking 40 individual stocks of S&P CNX Nifty. Using pair wise Granger Causality test, they found bidirectional causality in all the stocks of automobile sector except one i.e. Tata Motors. In banking sector seven out of nine stocks showed bidirectional causality. Out of the seven stocks of Gas, Oil and Refineries sector, only four stocks exhibited bidirectional causality. Similarly, bidirectional causality is also observed between the spot and futures markets of all six Pharmaceuticals stocks. However, in cement sector unidirectional causality is found except ACC which does not show causality. These findings are specifically important for stock exchange officials in designing the trading mechanism and contracts specification of Derivatives contracts.

Ali and Gupta (2011) tested the significance of hypothesis that futures prices are unbiased predictors of spot prices by taking 12 commodities traded on NCDEX of India. The result of the cointegration test showed the presence of long-term relationship in all ten commodities except wheat and rice. In short-run, futures market was found to act as a predictor of spot prices for wheat, castor seed, chickpea, guar seed, soybean, and sugar as compared to black lentil, maize, and pepper where bidirectional causality was observed. In case of rice, red lentil and cashew, futures market was lagging the spot market.

Abuk (2011) studied lead-lag relationship between the ISE 30 spot and futures indices of Turkey over the period of 5 years and 10 months using 5 minute intraday data. To empirically test the objective, the author applied Cointegration and Causality tests. To check the robustness of the result, the author used both the raw prices and filtered prices (using ARIMA) of the index. The study found that futures market led the spot market in 2008 and 2010, whereas bidirectional causality was observed in 2006, 2007 and 2009.

Jiang, Chang and Chiang (2012) employed the Autoregressive distributed lag cointegration framework (ARDL-ECM) for examining the intraday dynamic relationship between TAIEX stock index, TAIEX futures index and mini-TAIEX futures traded on Taiwan stock exchange. Using data from January to September 2004, they concluded that there exists unidirectional lead-lag relationship between futures and spot markets. They reported that futures market leads the spot market by about 30 minutes.

Kovalchak (2012) used 5-minute intraday data and employed three-stage-least-square regression to estimate the possible lead-lag relationship between the derivatives and cash markets of Russia. Although a bidirectional relationship was reported in the study, but during the time of expiration of the futures contracts, only recent movements in the one market are important for determining the future direction of the another market. In other words, this relationship tends to decline when futures contracts approaches expiration.

Mall, Bal and Mishra (2012) undertook a study on Indian Market by taking Nifty futures and cash indices. Their daily data of 10 years confirmed the presence of long-run relationship. They reported that futures market leads the spot market over the period of June, 2000 to May, 2011.

Srinivasan (2012) conducted an empirical study on Indian Commodities Market (MCX) by taking four spot and futures indices traded on it. The empirical results obtained provide evidence in support of the dominant role of commodities spot market over the futures market of all four indices in the matter of price discovery.

Yang, Yang and Zhou (2012) studied the price discovery between CSI 300 index and associated futures index in China. They used 5-min data from April 16, 2010 to July 30, 2010 and reported that spot market play a dominant role in price discovery. They ascribed leading role of spot market to restrictions in the futures market.

Srinivasan and Ibrahim (2012) examined the lead-lag relationship between the Gold spot and futures market traded on National Commodity Derivatives Exchange (NCDEX) of India. The results evidenced the leading role of Gold spot market over Gold futures market.

Choudhary and Bajaj (2012) employed VECM and Granger Causality test for studying the informational efficiency of spot and futures markets in India. They analyzed 5-min intraday data from April 2010 to March 2011 for CNX Nifty and 31 individual stocks. Their results indicate that price discovery takes place in both the markets, however, the role of futures market is more prominent.

Dey and Maitra (2012) explored the price discovery mechanism of commodities futures market using a series of econometric techniques- Granger causality, J-J cointegration, VECM, error correction with weak exogeneity, and forecast error variance decomposition tests. The results of the tests reported that there is unidirectional causality from futures to spot.

Theissen (2012) employed a modified Threshold Error Correction Model (TECM) to account for dynamic transaction costs for examining the price discovery roles of spot and futures markets. He investigated the relationship between DAX index and DAX index futures using data for the quarter of 1999. Besides, the relationship was also examined between DAX-EX (the most liquid ETF in Germany) and DAX futures employing data from the last quarter of 2010. Using midquotes data, he empirically demonstrated that futures market is informationally more efficient than the spot market. In the presence of arbitrage opportunities, he reported that DAX futures leads the underlying index, however, DAX-EX leading role over DAX futures is found to be stronger.

Stoyu I. Ivano (2013) examined the relationship between gold, silver and oil exchange traded funds (ETFs), their futures instrument and underlying commodities by using intradaily data. It was found that due to presence of ETFs, price discovery shifted from futures to ETFs for gold and silver commodities only, whereas for oil still price discovery takes place in futures market but with increased role of Oil ETF.

Sehgal, Rajput and Florent-Deisting (2013) in their study of intertemporal relation between the derivatives and its underlying used twelve commodities belonging to agricultural, metal and energy products (Chana, Gold, Naturalgas, Guar Seed, Silver, Crudeoil, Soybean, Zinc, Kapas, Lead, Potato Agra, Copper) as well as commodity indices (Mcx-Comdex, Mcx-Agri-Index, Mcx-Metal-Index and Mcx-Energy-Index) actively traded on Multi Commodity Exchange (MCX). The results indicate that there exists a long run equilibrium relationship among the spot and futures indices of 8 out of 12 commodities and in case of 3 indices out of four. It was also found that if the spot and futures markets deviated from their long term equilibrium level, they tend to adjust themselves to re-establish equilibrium. This was mostly found with 10 commodities whose spot prices make greater adjustment in order to re-establish the equilibrium level. Although there is bi-directional lead relationship between spot and futures in the MCX-Energy Index, Chana, Lead, Zinc, Copper, Crude Oil and single lead relationship in case of MCX-Condex Index, generally the results confirm the price discovery role of futures markets of most of the commodities.

Ersoy and Bayrakdaroglu (2013) undertook a study using Istanbul stock cash index and its futures contract, and determine that there is bidirectional causality between both the markets but no significant lead-lag relationship was observed. They also reported that both the markets were cointegrated.

Chauhan, Singh and Arora (2013) made an attempt to analyse the price discovery function of Indian Agri Commodities market using sample data of Guar Seed and Chana. In case of Gaur seed, they found bidirectional flow of information between spot and futures with futures market playing a dominant role in terms of price discovery. On the other hand, unidirectional causality is observed in case of Chana.

Chhajed and Mehta (2013) had taken nine commodities traded on MCX and NCDEX in India on which futures are available, in order to study their market behaviour and price discovery function. Price discovery was found to be effective for most of the commodities. They stated that the causality effect can be used to hedge or speculate on futures prices. Except for the two commodities, all other commodities showed significant effect of futures prices on spot prices.

Edward J and Rao TV (2013) reported the price discovery and causality presented in Turmeric futures and spot traded on NCDEX of India. They divided the sample period 1 April, 2007 to 31 March, 2013 into three sub-periods representing separate panels of data. The results suggested that there is no lead-lag relationship between the markets of Turmeric spot and futures.

Kumar and Chaturvedula (2013) employed the information share (implicit price) approach suggested by Hasbrouck (1995) for studying the contribution of Nifty spot and futures indices in price discovery. They found that the information share of futures and spot markets is 36% and 64% respectively.

Mishra, Malik and Pore (2013) addressed the issues of price discovery in futures, options and spot market of NSE of nifty index and ten selected stocks traded on Nifty index plus price discovery among futures and options markets under three different regimes of Securities Transaction Tax. By using the synchronous daily prices of spot, futures and options of stocks, they found the increasing role of spot over the derivatives market (futures and option), followed by decreasing role of futures over option with increase Securities Transaction Tax.

Choudhury and Bajaj (2013) investigated the price discovery function in Indian futures and spot markets by considering Nifty index and 41 individual stocks. Using daily data, they found that price discovery takes place in both the markets but futures market play a dominant role.

Hou and Li (2013) employed 5-min data from March 1, 2011 to March 31, 2011 for studying the price discovery roles of CSI 300 index and associated futures contracts in China. Their study found that futures market serves as a price discovery vehicle. Their findings are in sharp contrast to Yand et al. (2012) who reported dominant role of spot market.

Ullah and Shah (2013) examined the lead-lag relationship between spot and futures markets in Pakistan. They used daily data from 1995 to 2012 for 140 firms and concluded that futures market is more informationally efficient and largely performs the price discovery function.

Atif and Naseem (2014) used 1-min data for examining the lead-lag relationship between CNX Nifty and CNX Nifty futures. Using VECM and Granger causality test, they found that price discovery happens in both the markets, however, futures market play a stronger role.

2.2 STUDIES ON VOLATILITY SPILLOVERS BETWEEN SPOT AND FUTURES MARKETS

Chan, Chan and Karolyi (1991) investigated the 5-min intraday temporal relationship between the spot and index futures market of S&P 500 from 1984 to 1989. They found evidence of presence of strong inter market linkage in the volatility of both the markets. Using a bivariate GARCH model with AR (1)-GARCH (1,3) specification, they reported that price innovations in either of the market is helpful in predicting the futures volatility in the other market.

Using hourly data from 1986 to 1990, **Abhyankar (1995)** empirically examined the volatility relationships between FT-SE futures index and the underlying cash index. Using an EGARCH model, he first estimated two series of conditional variance for cash and futures markets and subsequently used these conditional variance in the framework of multiple regression to examine volatility linkages and predictive power of volatility in one market for volatility in the other market. He reported that there is no evidence of a systematic pattern of lead-lag in volatility. He further concluded that the tests for lead-lag based on the conditional estimates of volatility do not reveal any significant consistent leading behavior of one market over other during varying market conditions.

Using hourly data **Crain and Lee (1995)** examined the impact of scheduled macroeconomic announcements on the futures and spot markets of Eurodollar and Deutsche mark. They employed Granger Causality test based on VAR and found clear evidence that volatility in futures market leads volatility in spot market, however, no causality from spot to futures is reported.

Koutmos (1996) examined the returns and volatility linkages among the four major European stock markets namely, UK, Germany, France and Italy by employing a multivariate VAR-EGARCH model. The major contribution of the study is the extension of univariate EGARCH model into its multivariate counterpart. This model allows for studying the asymmetric influence of standardized Innovations in own as well as cross-markets on conditional volatility in each market. Using daily data from January, 1986 to December, 1991, the study found that there exists asymmetric volatility linkages among the four stock markets.

Koutmos and Tucker (1996) examined the second moment linkages, i.e. volatility spillovers between S&P 500 spot and futures indices. They used an error correction model (ECM) and allowed the residuals to follow a bivariate-EGARCH (1,1) process. Using daily data from April, 1984 to December, 1993, they found that volatility spillovers are unidirectional from futures to spot and not vice versa. Besides, volatility in each market was reported to be asymmetric in nature.

Huang, Masulis and Stoll (1996) investigated association between oil futures volatility and stock price volatility and found that oil futures volatility granger causes volatility in oil stocks and not vice versa.

Sim and Zurbreugg (1999) developed a quadvariate simultaneous-equation EC-ARCH model for the purpose of studying the intertemporal effects of the foreign cash and futures market upon the local cash market and local futures market in a single framework. Their study sought to determine the spillover effects of foreign stocks (Futures and Cash) on the domestic market (Futures and Cash). After analyzing the SPI futures and cash index and Nikkei 300 futures and cash index from July 24, 1997 to October 24, 1997, it was found that Australian futures is weak in price discovery process as compared to Japanese futures market. Further, it was found that volatility spillovers are uni-directional and runs from futures to cash market. They hypothesized that traders perception was formed in futures market (because of lower transaction cost and ease of trading) and later on transmitted to cash market in the form of volatility spillovers from futures to cash. They reported that the volatility in the Japanese futures market (Nikkie 300) first affects the Australian futures market and then Australian futures market in turn affects the Australian cash market. Thus, their study concluded that markets that are linked to international markets, a large part of spot-futures dynamics is affected by foreign market behavior.

Tse (1999) examined the volatility spillover mechanism of six months intraday data of DJIA futures and cash indices. For this purpose, he has used minute-by-minute cash and futures prices data for DJIA for the period from Nov 97 to Apr 98. Tse suggested a two step approach for studying volatility linkages in the two markets. In the first step, he estimated a VECM and obtained residuals. In the second step, he used bivariate-EGARCH with constant conditional correlations for studying volatility spillovers. Employing bivariate EGARCH, he concluded that both spot and futures markets innovations significantly affect volatility in the other market.

Min and Najund (1999) studied returns and volatility relationship between Kospi 200 index and associated futures contracts in Korea. They employed a VAR model and used absolute innovations from the returns equations as proxy for volatility in the two markets. Using 10-min intraday data from May to October 1996, they found that volatility interactions are interdependent in futures and spot markets.

Soydemir and Petrie (2003) examined intraday volatility transmission between the DJIA futures and spot markets. In their study, volatility series are derived using univariate GARCH models and later analysed in the framework of a VAR model. Using minute-by-minute data from March to August 1999, they found that there exists two way causality in returns volatility of spot and futures markets. However, futures market is reported to have greater impact on spot market.

Pok and Poshakwale (2004) undertook a study by taking the data of underlying stocks on which futures are available and non-underlying stocks on which futures trading is not available in Malaysian Stock Market. The study was conducted with the purpose of examining the impact of futures trading on volatility of spot market and determining the lead-lag and causal relationship between them. The study found that stocks on which futures contracts exist respond more quickly to new information than the stocks for which futures contracts do not exist. In addition, it is reported that trading in futures market causes spot market volatility with a lag of one day.

So and Tse (2004) examined the volatility spillovers among the three markets viz., the Hang Seng Index, the Hang Seng Index futures and Tracker fund. Using a multivariate GARCH model with 1-min data, they found that volatility spillovers run from futures to spot market and vice versa. Besides, it is also reported that volatility in the futures and spot market affect volatility of the Tracker fund but volatility in the Tracker fund does not affect volatility in the Hang Seng Index or the Hang Seng Index futures.

Using daily data from Mexican Securities markets, **Zhong, Darrat and Otero (2004)** examined volatility spillovers between IPC futures and the underlying cash index. Employing bivariate-EGARCH model with error correction term, they reported that innovations from either market affect volatility in other market.

Mukherjee and Mishra (2006) analyzed volatility spillovers between CNX Nifty futures and the underlying index as well as between futures and spot markets for five stocks. Using returns innovations as proxy for volatility in the context of a VAR model, they found that volatility spillovers run in both the directions, however, spillovers from spot to futures market are stronger.

Bose (2007) studied the characteristics of volatility in the spot and futures market in India. Volatility is found to exhibit the feature of mean reversion, volatility clustering, asymmetry and persistence in both spot and futures markets. Using daily data in the framework of the threshold GARCH model, she reported the leading role of futures market volatility over volatility in the spot market.

Kuo, Hsu and Chiang (2008) examined the volatility linkages between the Taiwan Stock Index and its associated contracts before and after the introduction of foreign investment (FI). The sample period is from July 21, 1998 to February 20, 2001 which is equally divided into pre and post foreign investment periods. By employing bivariate-EGARCH (1,1) model, they found that volatility spillovers are bidirectional in nature both before and after the participation of foreign investment. However, spillovers from futures to spot are larger in magnitude in the post FI period.

Using 1-min data from July to December 2006, **Mallikarjunappa and Afsal E M (2008)** have studied volatility linkages between futures and spot markets for 12 individual stocks in India. They used VECM-EGARCH (1,1) model and found that there exists bi-directional volatility spillovers between futures and spot markets. Besides, they also reported that volatility shocks are persistent and asymmetric in nature.

Using daily data from February, 2000 to June, 2003, **Kavussanos, Visvikis and Alexakis (2008)** investigated volatility spillovers between futures and spot markets in Greece. They examined volatility dynamics between FTSE/ATHEX-20 and underlying cash index and FTSE/ATHEX Mid-40 and its underlying cash index. Employing VECM-GARCH-X model, they reported that volatility spillovers run from futures to spot for both indices and not vice versa.

Lafuent-Luengo (2009) in their study employed realized volatility measure to empirically examine the dynamic relationship between market volatility of S&P 500 futures and its corresponding cash index. They used 15-min intraday data over the period from January 17, 2000 to November 26, 2002 and reported a unidirectional causal relationship of volatility from derivative market to cash market.

Karmakar (2009) used a bivariate-BEKK model for studying volatility spillovers between CNX Nifty and associated futures contracts. Using daily data, he reported that persistent volatility spillovers run bi-directionally. Further, he found that past innovations originating in the futures market have significant explanatory power for spot market volatility but past innovations from the spot market have no predictive power for futures market volatility.

Shakeel (2009) examined volatility linkages between Nifty and associated futures contracts. Using GARCH variance series as proxy for volatility, he found that volatility in the futures market affects spot market volatility and not vice versa.

Sakthival and Kamaiah (2010) used daily data from July 2001 through February 2008 for studying volatility spillovers between CNX Nifty futures and the underlying index. Using a TGARCH model, they found that volatility spillover takes place in both directions, however, futures market volatility is found to have greater influence on spot market volatility.

Wang and Ho (2010) used the data from 2 January, 2004 to 28 April, 2006 to examine the volatility relation between the underlying cash index, near-month and near-quarter TAIFEX index futures. The results based on GARCH model and Granger Causality test revealed that one-way volatility spillover takes place from futures to cash market and two-way spillovers run between the near-month futures contracts and near-quarter futures contracts.

Pati and Rajib (2011) used 5-min intraday data for studying lead-lag relationship for returns and volatility between CNX Nifty and CNX Nifty futures. Using a bivariate-GARCH (1,1) model with BEKK parameterization, they found that volatility transmissions occur in both the directions, however, the effect of futures market is more pronounced.

Srinivasan and Ibrahim (2012) examined lead-lag and volatility interactions between gold futures and spot markets in India. Using daily data from April, 2009 to May, 2011 and employing two step VECM-EGARCH suggested by Tse (1999), they found that gold spot market dominates price discovery. However, volatility linkages are reported to be bidirectional with futures market showing stronger spillover effects.

Yang, Yang and Zhou (2012) examined the 5-min intraday volatility transmission mechanism between CSI 300 index and associated futures index in China. They employed an asymmetric ECM-GARCH model and concluded that volatility in one market affects volatility in the other market.

Kang, Cheong and Yoon (2013) used intraday data of KOSPI 200 cash and futures indices to study the volatility spillover mechanism between the two markets. By employing bivariate GARCH-BEKK model they found that there is a bidirectional spillover of volatility between the two markets.

Chauhan, Singh and Arora (2013) examined the spillover effects between the cash market and the futures markets for three commodities, viz., Guar Seed and Chana. They found evidence confirming that the flow of information between spot and futures is bidirectional with futures market showing stronger spillovers in case of Guar seed. Further, in case of Chana, unidirectional causality is reported with spot volatility influencing the volatility in the futures market.

Sehgal, Rajput and Florent-Deisting (2013) studied intertemporal relation between the commodity derivatives and the underlying spot markets by using twelve commodities belonging to agricultural, metal and energy products (Chana, Gold, Naturalgas, Guar Seed, Silver, Crude oil, Soybean, Zinc, Kapas, Lead, Potato Agra, Copper) as well as 4 commodity indices (Mcx-Comdex, Mcx-Agri-Index, Mcx-Metal-Index and Mcx-Energy-Index) actively traded on Multi Commodity Exchange (MCX). They reported bidirectional volatility spillovers from spot to futures for three commodities namely- Soyabean, Zinc, and Natural Gas, whereas, no significant volatility spillovers were found in case of other commodities.

Rajput, Kakkar and Batra (2013) used daily data from June, 2000 through March, 2012 to examine volatility spillovers between Nifty and Nifty futures. Employing a bivariate-EGARCH model, the study provided evidence that CNX Nifty leads the Nifty futures in terms of price discovery and volatility spillovers. They reported unidirectional volatility spillovers from spot to futures with persistent volatility being bidirectional. Their results are in sharp contrast to many previous studies. However, they employed daily data and volatility dynamics are best studied with intraday data.

Kim and Ryu (2013) investigated the intraday volatility relationship among the KOSPI200 index, KOSPI200 futures index, and VKOSPI (implied volatility index). They employed a VAR (1) model with errors following a multivariate GARCH distribution with BEKK parameterization with asymmetry, i.e., VAR(1)-asymmetric-BEKK-GARCH(1,1). They found bidirectional volatility linkages between futures and spot markets with innovations in futures market having greater influence on spot market volatility.

2.3 <u>CONCLUSION</u>

Of all the studies reviewed in this chapter, most relate to equity derivatives and a few are concerned with commodity derivatives. Almost all the studies have found the leading role of futures market over the underlying spot market. It is reported that lead from futures to spot is by 10 to 50 minutes i.e. Kawaller, Koch and Koch (1987), Pizzi, Economopoulos and O'Neill (1998), Min and Najund (1999), Pok and Poshakwale (2004), Bhatia (2007), Gupta and Sing (2009), Abuk (2011) and Jiang, Chang and Chiang (2012). However, a few studies have also reported the leadership of spot market. Further, most of the studies supporting the leading role of spot market have employed daily data and it is well documented that for uncovering the dynamics of lead-lag relationship in financial markets intraday data is required.

Most of the studies supported bidirectional flow of information but Ng (1987), Ghosh (1993), Jong and Donders (1998), Pok and Poshakwale (2004), Lafuente-Luengo (2009), Ali and Gupta (2011), Jiang, Pati and Rajib (2011), Chang and Chiang (2012),

Srinivasan and Ibrahim (2012), Dey and Maitra (2012) and Rajput, Kakkar and Batra (2013) provided evidence in favor of unidirectional causality.

Review of literature reveals that to examine price discovery and lead-lag relationship, Multiple Regression, Correlation, J-J Cointegration, Granger Causality, Engle-Granger Error Correction Model, Vector error correction model, Impulse response function and Variance Decomposition function are the most popular methologies used. However, Tse (1999), Roope and Zurbruegg (2002), So and Tse (2004), Covrig, Ding and Low (2004), Stoyu I Ivano (2013) and Kumar and Chaturvedula (2013) among others employed Hasbrouk (1995) methodology of information share. Besides, Chan and Lien (2001), Lien and Yang (2003), and Mukherjee and Mishra (2006) used Gweke Feedback measures for examining the temporal relationship between futures and spot markets.

For volatility spillovers, most of the studies found bidirectional relationship between the two markets. However, spillovers from futures to spot market were reported to be stronger than in the reverse direction. VAR based Granger Causality and Bivariate/Multivariate-GARCH family of models were mostly employed for uncovering volatility interactions.

From the above discussion, it is clear that there is voluminous literature on first-moment i.e., returns relationship between futures and spot markets. However, second-moment i.e., volatility relationship is still under researched. Besides, a close scrutiny of the above studies reveals that in India most of the studies have used daily data which is of little use for understanding market micro-structure and cannot provide useful information to traders and arbitrageurs. In addition, most of the previous studies are confined to the analysis of index spot and futures relationship.

Overall, the review of literature provides the following research gap:

- Use of high frequency data

- Analysis of individual stocks

- Volatility interactions

The present study is an attempt to fill this gap by empirically investigating the dynamic interactions and interdependence of the spot market and the futures market returns for CNX Nifty and all its component stocks.

Chapter- 3
Research Methodology

The present chapter has five sections. Section 3.1 presents the objectives of the study; section 3.2 discusses the hypotheses to be tested; section 3.3 describes data used; section 3.4 describes methodology employed for achieving the stated objectives; and section 3.5 concludes.

3.1 OBJECTIVES OF THE STUDY

In the last few decades, enormous literature has been produced concerning relationships between futures and spot markets. Chapter 2 of the present study reviews an extensive literature survey of these studies. Most of these studies have examined lead-lag relationship between a market index and its associated futures contracts. Some studies have also investigated volatility linkages between the two markets viz., futures and spot markets. However, only a few studies have investigated lead-lag relationship and volatility spillovers at the level of individual stocks. The present study is an attempt to fill this gap to some extent.

The study is an attempt to examine first and second moments relationships between spot and futures markets in India. More specifically, the main objectives of the study are as follows:

1. To examine long-term relationship between futures and spot markets.
2. To examine lead-lag relationship for returns between futures and spot markets.
3. To examine volatility spillovers between futures and spot markets.
4. To examine the nature and strength of relationship between futures and spot markets.

3.2 HYPOTHESES OF THE STUDY

The present study requires a number of hypotheses to be tested. The major hypotheses to be tested are given below in the statistical form:

Long-term Relationship between Futures and Spot Markets-

H_0: There is no cointegration between futures and spot markets.

H_a: Futures and spot markets are cointegrated.

Lead-lag Relationships between Futures and Spot Markets-

H_0: Spot market (returns) does not granger cause futures market (returns).

H_a: Spot market (returns) granger causes futures market (returns).

H_0: Futures market (returns) does not granger cause spot market (returns).

H_a: Futures market (returns) granger causes spot market (returns).

Volatility Spillovers between Futures and Spot Markets-

H_0: Volatility from one market does not spill over to the other market.

H_a: Volatility from one market spills over to the other market.

The above stated hypotheses are tested for CNX Nifty and CNX Nifty Futures as well as for all of their 50 constituent stocks.

3.3 DATA

One of the primary objectives of the present study is to examine relationships between spot and futures markets in India. Generally, spot and futures markets relationships are studied at returns and volatility levels. For returns relationships, the primary concern is to investigate which market reacts to restore long-term equilibrium relationship and whether there exists any lead-lag relationship between the two markets. It is commonly known that lead-lag relationship between spot and futures markets which does not last for more than half an hour. Therefore, to study lead-lag relations, it is necessary that high frequency data should be used. The present study has used 5-min transaction prices data for CNX Nifty and all of its fifty constituent stocks. The data has been obtained from National Stock Exchange's data vending partner Dotex International Ltd. For the present study, one year data from 1st June 2012 to 31st May 2013 has been used. The reason for choosing this time period is that when the data was obtained then it was the latest data available with the data provider. In the time period considered there were a total of 250 trading days. Out of these days, 3 special trading sessions (2 on Sunday and 1 on Diwali) and one unusual[1] day has been removed. Thus, after excluding the four special/unusual days, data for 246 days have been used for carrying out the study.

The stocks used in the study are given in Table 3.1. NSE maintains a database of every single trade that takes place both in the cash market as well as in the derivatives market. From this database, 5-minutes transactions data has been filtered using R-

---

[1] September 08, 2012 (Saturday), November 13, 2012 (Diwali) and May 11, 2013 (Saturday) were special trading sessions.

software. For futures market, data for three different time periods is available viz. 1-month (nearby month), 2-month (mid-month), and 3-month (far-month). Since the nearby contracts are more liquid and usually most actively traded, only data for the nearby contracts has been used.

Table 3.1: Components of CNX Nifty as on 1st June 2012-

S.No.	Symbol	Stock
1	ACC	ACC Ltd.
2	AMBUJACEM	Ambuja Cements Ltd.
3	AXISBANK	Axis Bank Ltd.
4	BAJAJ-AUTO	Bajaj Auto Ltd.
5	BHARTIARTL	Bharti Airtel Ltd.
6	BHEL	Bharat Heavy Electricals Ltd.
7	BPCL	Bharat Petroleum Corporation Ltd.
8	CAIRN	Cairn India Ltd.
9	CIPLA	Cipla Ltd.
10	COALINDIA	Coal India Ltd.
11	DLF	DLF Ltd.
12	DRREDDY	Dr. Reddy's Laboratories Ltd.
13	GAIL	GAIL (India) Ltd.
14	GRASIM	Grasim Industries Ltd.
15	HCLTECH	HCL Technologies Ltd.
16	HDFC	Housing Development Finance Corporation Ltd.
17	HDFCBANK	HDFC Bank Ltd.
18	HEROMOTOCO	Hero MotoCorp Ltd.
19	HINDALCO	Hindalco Industries Ltd.
20	HINDUNILVR	Hindustan Unilever Ltd.
21	ICICIBANK	ICICI Bank Ltd.
22	IDFC	Infrastructure Development Finance Co. Ltd.
23	INFY	Infosys Ltd.
24	ITC	I T C Ltd.
25	JINDALSTEL	Jindal Steel & Power Ltd.
26	JPASSOCIAT	Jaiprakash Associates Ltd.
27	KOTAKBANK	Kotak Mahindra Bank Ltd.
28	LT	Larsen & Toubro Ltd.
29	M&M	Mahindra & Mahindra Ltd.
30	MARUTI	Maruti Suzuki India Ltd.
31	NTPC	NTPC Ltd.
32	ONGC	Oil & Natural Gas Corporation Ltd.
33	PNB	Punjab National Bank
34	POWERGRID	Power Grid Corporation of India Ltd.
35	RANBAXY	Ranbaxy Laboratories Ltd.

36	RCOM	Reliance Communications Ltd.
37	RELIANCE	Reliance Industries Ltd.
38	RELINFRA	Reliance Infrastructure Ltd.
39	RPOWER	Reliance Power Ltd.
40	SAIL	Steel Authority of India Ltd.
41	SBIN	State Bank of India
42	SESAGOA	Sesa Goa Ltd.
43	SIEMENS	Siemens Ltd.
44	STER	Sterlite Industries (India) Ltd.
45	SUNPHARMA	Sun Pharmaceutical Industries Ltd.
46	TATAMOTORS	Tata Motors Ltd.
47	TATAPOWER	Tata Power Co. Ltd.
48	TATASTEEL	Tata Steel Ltd.
49	TCS	Tata Consultancy Services Ltd.
50	WIPRO	Wipro Ltd.

Source: www.nseindia.com

3.4 METHODOLOGY

This section describes the methodology used to achieve the stated objectives of the study.

3.4.1 Methodology for Examining Returns Relationship between Spot and Futures Markets-

In this section methodology for studying returns relationship between spot and futures markets of CNX Nifty and its component stocks has been described.

Testing for Unit root-

Most of the economic and financial time series are unit root non-stationary. Further, most of these series have a single unit root. Series which have a single unit root become stationary after differencing once. Non-stationary series which become stationary after differencing once are called integrated of order one, i.e., I(1). Generally, a linear combination of integrated series is also integrated of the same order. However, the Granger representation theorem (1987) states that linear combination of non-stationary I(1) series may be stationary i.e., I(0). Hence, for studying cointegration, the first step is to test the time series under consideration for their order of integration. For this purpose Augmented Dickey-Fuller (ADF) test (Dickey & Fuller 1979) has been used. The test equation for ADF is given below:

$$y_t = \alpha_0 + \psi y_{t-1} + \sum_{i=1}^{p} \alpha_i \ y_{t-i} + \varepsilon_t \ldots\ldots\ldots\ldots\ldots\ldots (3.1)$$

In the above eq. if $\psi = 0$, then the series y_t is unit root non-stationary. As mentioned in Brooks (2008), owing to inherent instability of a non-stationary process, the usual t-statistics are no longer valid, therefore, to test whether $\psi = 0$, the critical values are derived from simulation. The critical values for ADF test based on simulation studies were tabulated by Dickey and Fuller (1979).

Cointegration and error correction model-

In a no arbitrage world there should be a long-term equilibrium relationship between spot and futures markets for any asset. If the series under consideration have a long-term equilibrium relationship which negates any arbitrage opportunity then it is said that such series are cointegrated. This long-run relationship or so called cointegration binds the series together and prevents them from wandering apart too far away. Though in the short-run, the series may deviate from each other, but arbitrage forces ensure that this deviation is corrected and the long-run equilibrium relationship is restored. Absence of cointegration implies that there is no long-term relationship between the series and they can very well wander apart without any bound. Since spot and futures prices represent prices of the same asset at two different points in time, they are expected to be cointegrated.

Let there be an m-dimensional vector y_t, $(y_{1t}, y_{2t}, ..., y_{mt})'$. If all the elements in y_t are stationary i.e., I(0), then a VAR could be set up containing p-lags of each of the variables in y_t as follows—

$$\underset{m \times 1}{y_t} = \underset{m \times m}{\beta_1} \underset{m \times 1}{y_{t-1}} + \underset{m \times m}{\beta_2} \underset{m \times 1}{y_{t-2}} + \cdots + \underset{m \times m}{\beta_p} \underset{m \times 1}{y_{t-p}} + \underset{m \times 1}{\varepsilon_t} \, \ldots \ldots \ldots (3.2)$$

However, if all the elements in y_t above are I(1), then the above VAR(p) model is meaningless. If the number of components in a system is more than the number of unit roots in the system, then the system is said to be cointegrated. Differencing each of the individual components of y_t to induce stationarity would result in over-differencing which creates problem of non-invertibility due to unit root introduced in its MA structure which in turn may lead to difficulties in parameter estimation (Tsay, 2010, p. 431). To overcome the problem of over-differencing, Engle and Granger (1987) suggested a transformation of the above Vector Autoregressive (VAR) model into an Error Correction Model (ECM). ECM exists if all the elements in y_t are I(1) and at least one linear combination of these elements is stationary i.e., I(0). The transformed model is given below—

$$y_t = \prod y_{t-1} + \Gamma_1 \, y_{t-1} + \cdots + \Gamma_{p-1} \, y_{t-(p-1)} + \varepsilon_t \ldots \ldots \ldots \ldots \ldots (3.3)$$

Where,

$$\prod = \left(\sum_{i=1}^{p} \beta_i \right) - I_m \quad and \quad \Gamma_i = -\sum_{j=i+1}^{p} \beta_j \qquad [where \ i = 1, 2, ..., p-1]$$

I_m is an m-dimensional square identity matrix.

Further, in the above specification can be represented as the product of two matrices α and β′ i.e., = αβ′. Replacing by αβ′ the above model can be written as follows:

$$y_t = \alpha\beta^{'y_{t-1}} + {}_1 \; y_{t-1} + \cdots + {}_{p-1} \; y_{t-(p-1)} + \varepsilon_t \; \ldots \ldots \ldots \ldots \ldots \ldots (3.4)$$

It is to be noted that in the above specification all the terms are stationary. y_t and all y $_{t-i}$ are stationary, since y_t is I(1) and hence its first difference is stationary. Besides, the expression $\beta'y_{t-1}$ is a linear combination of the components of y_t which is stationary. If no linear combination of the elements of y_t is stationary, then there is no cointegration. In that case, the usual first difference of each of the components of y_t would be used in a VAR model and no Error Correction Model (ECM) exists. For a cointegrated m-dimensional vector time series y_t with r cointegrating relations, α and β are m × r matrices of full rank.

There are many ways in which an error correction model can be constructed. In fact, Tsay (2010) has mentioned that one can use any $\alpha\beta'y_{t-s}$ for $1 \leq s \leq p$ with some modifications made to the coefficient matrices $_i$. For example, the above VECM can also be represented as follows—

$$y_t = {} \; y_{t-p} + {}_1 \; y_{t-1} + {}_2 \; y_{t-2} + \cdots + {}_{p-1} \; y_{t-(p-1)} + \varepsilon_t \; \ldots \ldots \ldots \ldots (3.5)$$

Where,

$$= \left(\sum_{i=1}^{p} \beta_i \right) - I_m \quad and \quad {}_i = \left(\sum_{j=1}^{i} \beta_j \right) - I_m$$

$$y_t = y_t - y_{t-1}$$

a nd $_i$ are m×m coefficient matrices

Testing for cointegration-

Once it is found that the time series believed to be cointegrated are I(1), the next step is to test whether these series are cointegrated or not. For this purpose, Johansen-Juselius (1990) cointegration procedure has been employed. The J-J procedure is described below:

Johansen-Juselius Procedure for Cointegration Analysis-

Let y_t be an m-dimensional time series whose components are I(1). If it is thought that the components of the y_t are cointegrated, then a Vector Error Correction Model (VECM) of the following form can be set up—

$$y_t = \; y_{t-p} + \; _1 \; y_{t-1} + \; _2 \; y_{t-2} + \cdots + \; _{p-1} \; y_{t-(p-1)} + \varepsilon_t \ldots \ldots \ldots (3.6)$$

Johansen test for cointegration among the elements of y_t is performed by examining the rank of the   matrix in the VECM above. Brooks (2008) mentioned that rank of the   matrix is examined by eigenvalues derived from rank-restricted moment matrices. Johansen (1988) has proposed two likelihood ratio test statistics, namely trace, and maximum eigenvalue for examining the rank of the m atrix.

1. Trace cointegration Test-

Johansen (1988) proposed a joint test, called Trace test, to determine the number of cointegrating vectors. Under trace test the null and alternative hypotheses are as follows:

H_0: rank ( ) = r; H_a: rank ( ) > r

Where, r = number of cointegrating vectors

The trace statistic is formulated as follows:

$$\lambda_{trace}(r) = -(T-p) \sum_{i=r+1}^{m} \ln\left(1-\hat{\lambda}_i\right) \dots\dots\dots\dots\dots (3.7)$$

2. *Maximum eigenvalue Test-*

Johansen (1988) also suggested a sequential procedure, called maximum eigenvalue test, to identify the number of cointegrating relations where separate tests are conducted on each eigenvalue. The null and alternative hypotheses under maximum eigenvalue test are as follows

H_0: rank ( ) = r; H_a: rank ( ) = r+1

Where, r = number of cointegrating vectors

The maximum eigenvalue test statistic is formulated as follows:

$$\lambda_{max}(r, r+1) = -T\ln\left(1-\hat{\lambda}_{r+1}\right) \dots\dots\dots\dots\dots\dots (3.8)$$

Johansen and Juselius (1990) have provided critical values for the two likelihood ratio test statistics. However, the distribution of λ_{trace} and λ_{max} statistics is non-standard and does not follow the usual chi-squared distribution, hence critical values for the tests are obtained via simulation.

Granger Causality-

At times, one might be interested in knowing whether changes in one variable cause changes in another variable. This question is addressed with the help of causality tests. Let y_t be a two-dimensional vector $(y_{1t}, y_{2t})'$. If history of y_{1t} is helpful in predicting y_{2t}, it is said that y_{1t} causes y_{2t}. Similarly, if past information about y_{2t} is useful for predicting y_{1t}, then y_{2t} is said to granger cause y_{1t}.

$$y_{1t} = \phi_{10} + \sum_{i=1}^{p} \alpha_i y_{1,t-i} + \sum_{i=1}^{p} \beta_i y_{2,t-i} + \epsilon_{1t} \dots\dots\dots\dots (3.9)$$

$$y_{2t} = \phi_{20} + \sum_{i=1}^{p} \gamma_i y_{1,t-i} + \sum_{i=1}^{p} \delta_i y_{2,t-i} + \epsilon_{2t} \dots \dots \dots \dots \dots (3.10)$$

In the above VAR model, equation for y_{1t} states that y_{1t} depends on its own past values plus past values of y_{2t}. However, if all β_i are jointly zero, then it would imply that y_2 does not cause y_1. Similarly, if all γ_i are jointly zero, then it would mean that y_1 does not cause y_2. If y_1 causes y_2 but not vice versa, then there is uni-directional flow of information from y_1 to y_2. If both y_1 and y_2 causes each other, then there is bi-directional flow of information and a feedback relationship is said to exist.

To perform Granger Causality test, two models are estimated-

1. *Unrestricted model for y_1.*

$$y_{1t} = \phi_{10} + \sum_{i=1}^{p} \alpha_i y_{1,t-i} + \sum_{i=1}^{p} \beta_i y_{2,t-i} + \epsilon_{1t} \dots \dots \dots \dots \dots \dots (3.11)$$

2. *Restricted model for y_1.*

$$y_{1t} = \phi_{10} + \sum_{i=1}^{p} y_{1,t-i} + \epsilon_{1t} \dots \dots \dots \dots \dots \dots \dots \dots (3.12)$$

In the second specification above, we have restricted all β_i i.e., lagged coefficients of $y_2 = 0$. This joint restriction that all β_i are simultaneously zero can be tested in the framework of an F-test as follows

$$F - test = \frac{\frac{RRSS - URSS}{p}}{\frac{URSS}{T - 2p}} \dots \dots \dots \dots \dots \dots (3.13)$$

Where,

URSS = residual sum of squares from unrestricted regression.

RRSS = residual sum of squares from restricted regression.

p = number of restrictions; here equal to number of lags of y_{2t}.

T = total number of observations.

2p = number of regressors in the unrestricted regression; here p lags of y_{1t} and p lags for y_{2t}.

The above test-statistic follows an F-distribution with p and T−2p degrees of freedom in numerator and denominator respectively. Similar procedure is followed for y_{2t}.

3.4.2 Methodology for studying volatility spillover between spot and futures markets-

For studying volatility spillovers between different time series, two approaches are commonly used-

1. Multivariate GARCH models

2. Granger causality based on Vector Autoregressive (VAR) models of squared returns or squared residuals.

Multivariate GARCH Model-

There is numerous literature which indicate that financial assets returns exhibit features of volatility clustering and time-varying conditional heteroscedasticity which is well captured by Autoregressive Conditional Heteroscedasticity (ARCH) and Generalised Autoregressive Conditional Heteroscedasticity (GARCH) type models. In spirit, multivariate GARCH models are very similar to univariate volatility models, except that they also model covariances. Furthermore, multivariate formulations of ARCH/GARCH models allow for examination of inter-market volatility linkages including volatility spillovers. In the literature, several formulations of Multivariate GARCH models have been proposed. The present study has used two different bivariate GARCH family of models given below-

1. *Bivariate GARCH (1,1)-*

The following bivariate GARCH (1,1) with student-t innovations has been used to examine volatility spillovers between the spot and futures markets.

$$\epsilon_t = \begin{bmatrix} \epsilon_{s,t} \\ \epsilon_{f,t} \end{bmatrix} \mid \Omega_{t-1} \sim Student - t(0, H_t, v) \dots\dots\dots\dots\dots\dots\dots (3.14)$$

$$H_t = \begin{bmatrix} \epsilon^2_{s,t} & \epsilon_{s,t}\,\epsilon_{f,t} \\ \epsilon_{f,t}\,\epsilon_{s,t} & \epsilon^2_{f,t} \end{bmatrix} \dots\dots\dots\dots\dots\dots\dots\dots (3.15)$$

$$\begin{bmatrix} \epsilon^2_{s,t} \\ \epsilon^2_{f,t} \end{bmatrix} = \begin{bmatrix} \omega_s \\ \omega_f \end{bmatrix} + \begin{bmatrix} \alpha_s & \gamma_f \\ \gamma_s & \alpha_f \end{bmatrix} \begin{bmatrix} \epsilon^2_{s,t-1} \\ \epsilon^2_{f,t-1} \end{bmatrix} + \begin{bmatrix} \beta_s & 0 \\ 0 & \beta_f \end{bmatrix} \begin{bmatrix} \sigma^2_{s,t-1} \\ \sigma^2_{f,t-1} \end{bmatrix} \dots\dots\dots\dots(3.16)$$

$$\sigma^2_{s,t} = \omega_s + \alpha_s\,\epsilon^2_{s,t-1} + \gamma_f\,\epsilon^2_{f,t-1} + \beta_s\,\sigma^2_{s,t-1} \dots\dots\dots\dots (3.17)$$

$$\sigma^2_{f,t} = \omega_f + \gamma_s\,\epsilon^2_{s,t-1} + \alpha_f\,\epsilon^2_{f,t-1} + \beta_f\,\sigma^2_{f,t-1} \dots\dots\dots\dots (3.18)$$

Where,

$\epsilon_{s,t}, \epsilon_{f,t}$ = residuals from VECM for the spot and futures markets respectively.

Ω_{t-1} = set of information available at time $t-1$.

H_t = variance-covariance matrix

v = degrees of freedom

ρ = coefficient of correlation between spot and futures markets.

$\sigma^2_{s,t}, \sigma^2_{f,t}$ = conditional variance for the spot and futures markets respectively.

The above sets of equations are jointly estimated by maximizing the following log likelihood function:

$$L(\ ) = \sum_{t=1}^{T} \ln\{I_t(\ )\} \dots \dots \dots \dots \dots \dots \dots (3.19)$$

$$I_t(\ ) = \frac{T[(2+v)/2]}{T(v/2)[\ (v-2)]} |H_t|^{-1/2} \left[1 \pm \frac{1}{v-2} \ '_t H_t^{-1} \ _t\right]^{-(2+v)/2} \dots \dots \dots \dots \dots (3.20)$$

In the conditional variance equation above α_s and α_f describe market specific volatility clustering for the spot and futures markets respectively. γ_f and γ_s measure volatility spillover from futures to spot market, and spot to futures market respectively. For modeling covariances, denotes constant conditional correlation as in Bollerslev (1990), Chan, Chan and Karolyi (1991), Tse (1999) among others. Student-t distribution has been used for capturing excessive kurtosis and fat tails commonly exhibited by returns of financial assets.

2. Bivariate EGARCH (1,1)-

To complement the results from bivariate GARCH (1,1), one more formulation of multivariate GARCH models has been employed. The model is bivariate EGARCH (1,1) used by Koutmos and Tucker (1996), Koutmos (1996) and Tse (1999) among others.

$$_t = \begin{bmatrix} s,t \\ f,t \end{bmatrix} | \ _{t-1} \sim \text{Student} - t(0, H_t, v), \dots \dots \dots \dots \dots (3.21)$$

$$H_t = \begin{bmatrix} \ ^2_{s,t} & s,t \ f,t \\ f,t \ s,t & \ ^2_{f,t} \end{bmatrix} \dots \dots \dots \dots \dots \dots \dots \dots \dots (3.22)$$

$$\ln(\ ^2_{st}) = \ _s + \alpha_s G_{s,t-1} + \gamma_f G_{f,t-1} + \beta_s \ln(\ ^2_{s,t-1}) \dots \dots \dots \dots \dots \dots \dots (3.23)$$

$$\ln\left(\sigma^2_{f,t}\right) = \omega_f + \gamma_s G_{s,t-1} + \alpha_f G_{f,t-1} + \beta_f \ln\left(\sigma^2_{f,t-1}\right) \dots \dots \dots \dots \dots \dots \dots (3.24)$$

$$G_{s,t-1} = \left(\left|\varepsilon_{s,t-1}\right| - E\left|\varepsilon_{s,t-1}\right|\right) + \delta_s \varepsilon_{s,t-1} \dots \dots \dots \dots \dots \dots \dots (3.25)$$

[where $\varepsilon_{s,t-1} = \eta_{s,t-1}/ \sigma_{s,t-1}$]

$$G_{f,t-1} = \left(\left|\varepsilon_{f,t-1}\right| - E\left|\varepsilon_{f,t-1}\right|\right) + \delta_f \varepsilon_{f,t-1} \dots \dots \dots \dots \dots \dots \dots (3.26)$$

[where $\varepsilon_{f,t-1} = \eta_{f,t-1}/ \sigma_{f,t-1}$]

Where,

$\varepsilon_{s,t-1}$ and $\varepsilon_{f,t-1}$ are standardized residuals for spot and futures markets respectively.

δ_s and δ_f are asymmetric coefficients for the spot and futures markets respectively.

Other symbols are defined in bivariate GARCH formulation above.

The bivariate-EGARCH above is estimated by maximizing the following log-likelihood function:

$$L(\theta) = -0.5(NT)\ln(2\pi) - 0.5 \sum_{t=1}^{T} \left(\ln|\Sigma_t| + \varepsilon'_t \Sigma_t^{-1}\varepsilon_t\right) \dots \dots \dots \dots \dots \dots . (3.27)$$

Where,

N = number of equations (two in the present case)

T = number of observations

$\varepsilon'_t = [\varepsilon_{st}, \varepsilon_{ft}]$ 1×2 vector of innovations at time t

$\Sigma_t =$ time − varying comditional variance − covariance matrix of innovations

Volatility Spillover based on VAR-

To complement the results from GARCH family of models, the present study has also examined volatility spillover in the framework of a vector autoregressive (VAR) model. The following bivariate-VAR has been used—

$$\varepsilon_{s,t}^2 = \varepsilon_s + \sum_{i=1}^{k} \alpha_i \varepsilon_{s,t-i}^2 + \sum_{i=1}^{k} \beta_i \varepsilon_{f,t-1}^2 + \upsilon_{s,t} \quad \ldots\ldots\ldots\ldots\ldots\ldots\ldots (3.28)$$

$$\varepsilon_{f,t}^2 = \varepsilon_f + \sum_{i=1}^{k} \gamma_i \varepsilon_{s,t-1}^2 + \sum_{i=1}^{k} \delta_i \varepsilon_{f,t-1}^2 + \upsilon_{f,t} \ldots\ldots\ldots\ldots\ldots\ldots\ldots (3.29)$$

Where,

$\varepsilon_{s,t}^2, \varepsilon_{f,t}^2$ = residuals from VECM for spot and futures markets respectively

$\upsilon_{s,t}, \upsilon_{f,t}$ = white noise error terms

In the above formulation if all β_i are jointly found to be zero, then it would imply that there is no volatility spillover from futures to spot market. Similarly, if all γ_i are all jointly zero, it would mean that there is no volatility spillover from spot to futures market.

3.5 <u>CONCLUSION</u>

This chapter describes objectives and hypotheses of the study. Then, data and methodology used in the thesis to achieve the stated objectives are described. For studying the returns relationship between spot and futures markets, the study proposes to use Johansen cointegration analysis and Granger causality based on vector autoregression. For studying volatility spillovers between the two markets, the study proposes to use bivariate GARCH (1,1) and EGARCH (1,1) with constant conditional correlation. In addition, to complement the results from GARCH type models, volatility spillover is also to be studied in the framework of a VAR model.

Chapter-4
Empirical Evidence on Returns Relationship between Futures and Spot Markets

For efficient and frictionless markets, the spot and futures prices of a financial asset should react to new information simultaneously. This implies that there should not be any lead-lag relationship between the two markets. However, many research studies have documented that there exists lead-lag relationship between the spot and futures markets.

This chapter presents empirical evidence regarding error correction and lead-lag relationship between spot and futures markets for S&P CNX Nifty and its fifty constituent stocks.

The chapter is divided into three sections - Section 4.1 presents returns relationship between CNX Nifty and its associated futures index, section 4.2 presents returns relationship between spot and futures markets for 50 individual stocks and section 4.3 gives concluding remarks.

4.1 COINTEGRATION, ERROR-CORRECTION AND LEAD-LAG RELATIONSHIP BETWEEN CNX NIFTY AND CNX NIFTY FUTURES

Table 4.1 presents descriptive statistics for 5-min percentage returns for CNX Nifty (spot) and CNX Nifty Futures (futures) for the time period starting from 1st June 2012 to 31st May 2013. Mean return for both CNX Nifty and its futures index for the full sample period is 0.0012%. However, for the restricted sample mean return is approximately −0.0005% and 0.0002% for the spot and the futures market respectively. Standard deviation for both the series is almost same (0.09% for the full sample and 0.077% for the restricted sample) which indicates that CNX Nifty and its futures index are equally volatile. For the full sample, skewness is positive for both the spot and the futures market. For the restricted sample, skewness value of −0.1560 for spot market and −0.0685 for futures market reveals that both the series are negatively skewed, however the degree of asymmetry is low. Both the return series are highly leptokurtic as kurtosis for both the series is well above 3 for both the samples. Further, JB test of normality is rejected for both the series which indicates that the two return series under consideration are non-normal and have fat tails. In comparison to the restricted sample, kurtosis for the full sample which includes overnight returns is very high. This indicates that when markets open, there is large change in prices compared to the previous day's close.

Figure 4.1 and 4.2 plots 5-min transaction price data for CNX Nifty and its futures index for the full and the restricted samples respectively. In the top panel of the figures 4.1 and 4.2 log prices are plotted in their levels and in the lower panel first differences of log prices which are also continuously compounded returns are displayed. In order to construct a statistically appropriate model, the variables should first be examined as to whether they are stationary or not.

Table 4.1: Summary Statistics for CNX Nifty and CNX Nifty Futures-

	Full Sample		Restricted Sample	
	ΔS_t	ΔF_t	ΔS_t	ΔF_t
Observations	18449	18449	18203	18203
Mean	0.0012	0.0012	-0.0005	0.0003
Median	0.0000	0.0000	0.0000	0.0000
Maximum	1.9042	2.0384	0.8158	0.7533
Minimum	-1.0829	-1.1449	-0.8304	-0.7588
Std. Dev.	0.0928	0.0946	0.0766	0.0784
Skewness	1.6649	1.7363	-0.1560	-0.0685
Kurtosis	40.6554	48.2815	7.9327	9.0112
Jarque-Bera	1098496	1585443	18528	27420
Probability	0.0000	0.0000	0.0000	0.0000

[Notes: ΔS_t and ΔF_t are the first differences of logarithmic prices for Spot and Futures series respectively and represent continuously compounded returns for the respective markets.]

A visual examination of the figure 4.1 suggests that both CNX Nifty spot and futures series are non-stationary in their levels while their first differences are stationary. Figure 4.2 conveys the same thing for the restricted sample. Further, to supplement the graphical analysis, Augmented Dickey-Fuller (ADF) test has been employed on log levels and first differences of the two time series. The results of ADF test presented in Table 4.2 indicate that both the spot and futures price series are non-stationary in their levels and their first differences are stationary. Thus, as one would expect, log prices are non-stationary while returns are stationary. Hence, it can be concluded that both CNX Nifty and CNX Nifty Futures index are integrated of order 1 i.e., I(1). Since, statistical models of non-stationary variables are spurious, the appropriate way is to model returns. However, one problem with pure first difference models is that such models do not have any long-term solution. Moreover, theory suggests that the spot and futures prices should have long-term relationship.

Figure 4.1: 5-min time plot for CNX Nifty and CNX Nifty Futures for the period June 1, 2012 to May 31, 2013 (Full Sample)-

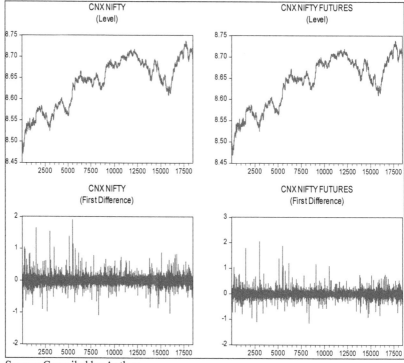

Source: Compiled by Author

Table 4.2: Augmented Dickey Fuller Test-

Variable	Full Sample		Restricted Sample	
	ADF test-Statistic	Prob.	ADF test-Statistic	Prob.
S_t	-2.1474	0.2261	-2.1737	0.2162
F_t	-2.2324	0.1948	-2.2490	0.1890
ΔS_t	-142.3372	0.0001	-142.0660	0.0001
ΔF_t	-138.4572	0.0001	-138.1040	0.0001

[Notes: For ADF test, the null hypothesis is that the series under consideration has a unit root i.e., non-stationary.]

Figure 4.2: 5-min time plot for CNX Nifty and CNX Nifty Futures for the period June 1, 2012 to May 31, 2013 (Restricted Sample)-

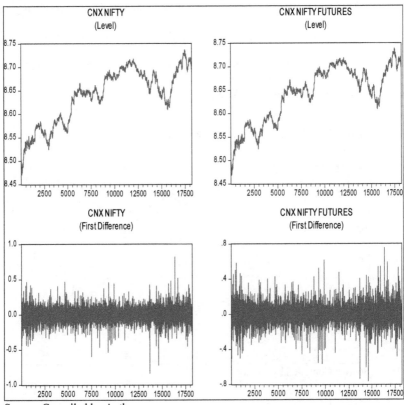

Source: Compiled by Author

Therefore, the next step is to examine whether there exists any cointegrating relationship between the two series. The efficient market hypothesis postulates that spot and futures price series should move closely and not wander too far away. Figure 4.3 displays the time plot of CNX Nifty and its associated futures contract for the restricted sample. It can be seen that the spot and the futures price series are moving together which implies that the two series may be cointegrated. Further, to test formally whether CNX Nifty and its futures contract are actually cointegrated, Johansen-Juselius (1990) cointegration analysis has been performed. Under the J-J (Johansen-Juselius) methodology two likelihood ratio test statistics namely trace and maximum eigenvalue are employed. The results of the trace and the maximum eigenvalue test are presented in Table 4.3. Trace test rejects the hypothesis of no cointegrating vector but fails to reject the hypothesis of one cointegrating vector at 1% level of significance. Similar results are obtained by applying maximum eigenvalue test. Hence, it can be concluded that for CNX Nifty, spot and futures price series are cointegrated of order (1,1).[1]

Figure 4.3: Time Plot of CNX Nifty and CNX Nifty Futures (combined)-

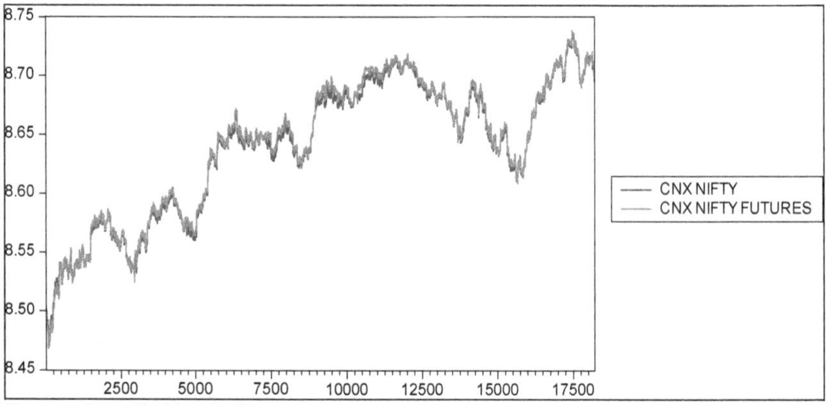

Source: Compiled by Author

Table 4.3: Cointegration Analysis (Restricted Sample)-

Unrestricted Cointegration Rank Test (Trace)				
Hypothesized No. of CE(s)	Eigenvalue	Trace Statistic	0.01 Critical Value	Prob.
None	0.0025	49.5675	19.9371	0.0000
At most 1	0.0003	4.6944	6.6349	0.0303
Unrestricted Cointegration Rank Test (Maximum Eigenvalue)				
Hypothesized No. of CE(s)	Eigenvalue	Max-Eigen Statistic	0.01 Critical Value	Prob.
None	0.0025	44.8731	18.5200	0.0000
At most 1	0.0003	4.6944	6.6349	0.0303

---

[1] The results of cointegration analysis for the full sample were almost similar and hence not presented here.

Having established that the spot and the futures series are cointegrated, the next step is to estimate error correction model following Granger representation theorem. Table 4.4 shows the estimates of Vector Error Correction Model (VECM) for the full sample based on the following specification:

$$\Delta S_t = \phi_s + \alpha_s ect_{t-1} + \sum_{i=1}^{k} \alpha_i \Delta S_{t-i} + \sum_{i=1}^{k} \beta_i \Delta F_{t-i} + \varepsilon_{s,t} \quad \dots\dots\dots (4.1a)$$

$$\Delta F_t = \phi_f + \alpha_f ect_{t-1} + \sum_{i=1}^{k} \gamma_i \Delta S_{t-i} + \sum_{i=1}^{k} \delta_i \Delta F_{t-i} + \varepsilon_{f,t} \quad \dots\dots\dots (4.1b)$$

Where,

$\Delta S_t = S_t - S_{t-1}$ i.e., first difference of log of spot prices

$\Delta F_t = F_t - F_{t-1}$ i.e., first difference of log of futures prices

ect_{t-1} = lagged residual term from potentially cointegrated regression, $S_t = \alpha_s + \beta F_t + ect_t$

ϕ_s, ϕ_f = constants

α_s, α_f = coefficient of the error correction term

α_i, β_i, γ_i and δ_i = coefficients of lagged terms

$\varepsilon_{s,t}$, $\varepsilon_{f,t}$ = residual term at time t

For estimating the VECM for the full sample, 3 lags are found most appropriate based on Schwarz Information Criterion (SIC). The estimates of the VECM are presented in Table 4.4.

Table 4.4: Estimates of VECM for CNX Nifty and CNX Nifty Futures (Full Sample)-

Variable	ΔS_t			ΔF_t		
	Coeff	Std Error	p-value	Coeff	Std Error	p-value
ect_{t-1}	-0.0020	0.0031	0.5153	0.0054*	0.0032	0.0911
ΔS_{t-1}	-0.2274**	0.0221	0.0000	0.0714**	0.0226	0.0016
ΔS_{t-2}	-0.0981**	0.0229	0.0000	0.0261	0.0234	0.2637
ΔS_{t-3}	-0.0379*	0.0220	0.0856	0.0173	0.0226	0.4442
ΔF_{t-1}	0.1883**	0.0216	0.0000	-0.0824**	0.0221	0.0002
ΔF_{t-2}	0.0878**	0.0222	0.0001	-0.0225	0.0227	0.3231
ΔF_{t-3}	0.0501**	0.0215	0.0196	0.0019	0.0220	0.9312
Constant	0.0012*	0.0007	0.0684	0.0012*	0.0007	0.0786

[Notes: ** and * denotes significance at 5% an 10% level respectively]

From the table it can be seen that the coefficient of the error correction term ect_{t-1} for ΔF_t is positive and statistically significant at 10% level. However, the error correction term for ΔS_t is statistically insignificant. It implies that futures market responds to correct for the disequilibrium from the long-term relationship and spot market does not. Further, the positive coefficient of ect_{t-1} for ΔF_t implies that if futures price is relatively lower than spot price at time $t-1$, then it is likely to adjust upward to restore the equilibrium in the next period. Moreover, for ΔS_t, own lags as well as lags of ΔF_t are statistically significant. However, for ΔF_t, neither own lags nor lags of ΔS_t are significant except for lag 1. It implies that for predicting spot market, information for the last 15 minutes (3 lags) is important, however, for the futures market, only last 5 minutes information (1 lag) is useful.

Some authors like Koutmos (1996), Tse (1999), Gupta and Singh (2009) and others have used basis for error correction term. Therefore, VECM based on basis has also been estimated and presented in Table 4.5. The eqs. for VECM based on basis are given below:

$$\Delta S_t = \phi_s + \alpha_s z_{t-1} + \sum_{i=1}^{k} \alpha_i \Delta S_{t-i} + \sum_{i=1}^{k} \beta_i \Delta F_{t-i} + \varepsilon_{s,t} \quad \dots\dots\dots (4.2a)$$

$$\Delta F_t = \phi_f + \alpha_f z_{t-1} + \sum_{i=1}^{k} \gamma_i \Delta S_{t-i} + \sum_{i=1}^{k} \delta_i \Delta F_{t-i} + \varepsilon_{f,t} \quad \dots\dots\dots (4.2b)$$

Where,

$\Delta S_t = S_t - S_{t-1}$ i.e., first difference of log of spot prices

$\Delta F_t = F_t - F_{t-1}$ i.e., first difference of log of futures prices

z_{t-1} = lagged basis term given by: $F_{t-1} - S_{t-1}$

ϕ_s, ϕ_f = constants

α_s, α_f = coefficient of the error correction term

α_i, β_i, γ_i and δ_i = coefficients of lagged terms

$\varepsilon_{s,t}$, $\varepsilon_{f,t}$ = residual term at time t

The results of utilizing basis as the error correction term in the VECM are qualitatively same. From the table 4.5, it can be seen that error correction term z_{t-1} for ΔF_t is negative and statistically significant implying that if in the immediately preceding time period futures price is more than spot price then futures market makes downward adjustment to restore the long-term equilibrium. Again, for ΔS_t, own lags as well as lags of futures market are statistically significant and for ΔF_t only the first lag is significant.

Table 4.5: Estimates of VECM for CNX Nifty and CNX Nifty Futures (Full Sample) using Basis-

Variable	ΔS_t			ΔF_t		
	Coeff	Std Error	p-value	Coeff	Std Error	p-value
Z_{t-1}	-0.0001	0.0030	0.9638	-0.0071**	0.0031	0.0206
ΔS_{t-1}	-0.2288**	0.0221	0.0000	0.0703**	0.0226	0.0019
ΔS_{t-2}	-0.0991**	0.0229	0.0000	0.0253	0.0234	0.2791
ΔS_{t-3}	-0.0387*	0.0220	0.0795	0.0167	0.0225	0.4599
ΔF_{t-1}	0.1897**	0.0216	0.0000	-0.0813**	0.0221	0.0002
ΔF_{t-2}	0.0889**	0.0222	0.0001	-0.0217	0.0227	0.3410
ΔF_{t-3}	0.0509**	0.0215	0.0178	0.0025	0.0220	0.9094
Constant	0.0013	0.0010	0.2020	0.003**	0.0010	0.0038

[Notes: ** and * denotes significance at 5% an 10% level respectively]

Table 4.6 and 4.7 presents the estimates of VECM for the restricted sample for eqs. 4.1 and 4.2 respectively. From the tables, it can be seen that the results from the restricted sample are qualitatively similar to that of the full sample. It is the futures market which is responsive to the deviation from the equilibrium relationship. However, size and significance of lagged coefficients suggest that spot market has a memory of 15 to 25 minutes but futures market has a memory of only 5 minutes.

Besides the above two samples namely full sample and restricted sample excluding overnight returns, one more VECM has been estimated after removing first and last 30-minutes of data to remove the effects of excessive trading at the open and close of trading hours. The fitted VECM is given in table 4.8. In this table, the basis term z_{t-1} is significant for both ΔS_t and ΔF_t which implies that error correction takes place in both the markets. Again, if we examine individual coefficients then for ΔS_t all the three lags from the spot and futures markets are significant, and for ΔF_t only one lag is significant. This indicates that for predicting futures market returns only past 5-min returns information from the spot market is important and any older information is not important.

Table 4.6: Estimates of VECM for CNX Nifty and CNX Nifty Futures (Restricted Sample)-

Variable	ΔS_t			ΔF_t		
	Coeff	Std Error	p-value	Coeff	Std Error	p-value
ect_{t-1}	0.0016	0.0026	0.5331	0.004	0.0027	0.1316
ΔS_{t-1}	-0.2556**	0.0224	0.0000	0.0865**	0.0230	0.0002
ΔS_{t-2}	-0.1731**	0.0235	0.0000	-0.0142	0.0242	0.5572
ΔS_{t-3}	-0.138**	0.0237	0.0000	-0.0488**	0.0244	0.0453
ΔS_{t-4}	-0.066**	0.0235	0.0050	-0.0048	0.0242	0.8422
ΔS_{t-5}	-0.0355	0.0223	0.1115	0.0087	0.0229	0.7046
ΔF_{t-1}	0.2044**	0.0218	0.0000	-0.1057**	0.0224	0.0000
ΔF_{t-2}	0.1654**	0.0228	0.0000	0.0267	0.0234	0.2535
ΔF_{t-3}	0.1445**	0.0229	0.0000	0.0645**	0.0235	0.0062
ΔF_{t-4}	0.0796**	0.0227	0.0005	0.0237	0.0234	0.3104
ΔF_{t-5}	0.0418*	0.0216	0.0534	0.0075	0.0222	0.7366
Constant	-0.001*	0.0006	0.0693	0.0003	0.0006	0.5952

[Notes: ** and * denotes significance at 5% an 10% level respectively]

Table 4.7: Estimates of VECM for CNX Nifty and CNX Nifty Futures (Restricted Sample) using Basis-

Variable	ΔS_t			ΔF_t		
	Coeff	Std Error	p-value	Coeff	Std Error	p-value
Z_{t-1}	-0.0035	0.0025	0.1679	-0.005*	0.0026	0.0513
ΔS_{t-1}	-0.2593**	0.0223	0.0000	0.0775**	0.0228	0.0007
ΔS_{t-2}	-0.1724**	0.0234	0.0000	-0.0152	0.0239	0.5252
ΔS_{t-3}	-0.1387**	0.0235	0.0000	-0.0486**	0.0241	0.0436
ΔS_{t-4}	-0.0843**	0.0233	0.0003	-0.0158	0.0239	0.5070
ΔS_{t-5}	-0.0399*	0.0222	0.0720	0.0065	0.0227	0.7762
ΔF_{t-1}	0.2081**	0.0217	0.0000	-0.0984**	0.0223	0.0000
ΔF_{t-2}	0.1659**	0.0227	0.0000	0.0280	0.0232	0.2270
ΔF_{t-3}	0.1463**	0.0228	0.0000	0.065**	0.0233	0.0053
ΔF_{t-4}	0.0946**	0.0226	0.0000	0.0330	0.0232	0.1542
ΔF_{t-5}	0.0448**	0.0216	0.0377	0.0093	0.0221	0.6732
Constant	-0.0002	0.0008	0.7682	0.0015*	0.0009	0.0830

[Notes: ** and * denotes significance at 5% an 10% level respectively]
[Z_{t-1} is the error correction term lagged one period]

Table 4.8: Estimates of VECM for CNX Nifty and CNX Nifty Futures (after removing first and last 30-minutes) using Basis-

Variable	ΔS_t			ΔF_t		
	Coeff	Std Error	p-value	Coeff	Std Error	p-value
Z_{t-1}	-0.0058**	0.0026	0.0249	-0.005*	0.0027	0.0634
ΔS_{t-1}	-0.3033**	0.0257	0.0000	0.0936**	0.0269	0.0005
ΔS_{t-2}	-0.1727**	0.0271	0.0000	0.0249	0.0284	0.3809
ΔS_{t-3}	-0.1302**	0.0257	0.0000	-0.03	0.0268	0.2644
ΔF_{t-1}	0.2452**	0.0246	0.0000	-0.1173**	0.0258	0.0000
ΔF_{t-2}	0.166**	0.0258	0.0000	-0.0099	0.0270	0.7146
ΔF_{t-3}	0.1262**	0.0245	0.0000	0.0401	0.0256	0.1174
const	0.0003	0.0009	0.7497	0.0015*	0.0009	0.0990

[Notes: ** and * denotes significance at 5% an 10% level respectively]
[Z_{t-1} is the error correction term lagged one period]

Further, to examine the direction of flow of information between spot and futures markets, Granger Causality test has been applied based on VAR and is presented in Table 4.9. The null hypothesis that futures market does not granger cause spot market is rejected at 5% level of significance for all the three samples. Similarly, the null hypothesis that spot market does not granger cause futures market is also rejected for all the sample specifications. It implies that for CNX Nifty, spot and futures markets have feedback relationship and significant information transmission takes place between the two markets.

Table 4.9: Granger Causality Test for CNX Nifty & CNX Nifty Futures-

Null Hypothesis	Sample 1		Sample 2		Sample 3	
	F-stat	p-value	F-stat	p-value	F-stat	p-value
ΔF_t does not Granger Cause ΔS_t	27.3775	0.0000	25.4916	0.0000	31.0233	0.0000
ΔS_t does not Granger Cause ΔF_t	3.7728	0.0101	4.6611	0.0003	4.1748	0.0022

[Notes: Sample 1 denotes the full sample; Sample 2 denotes sample obtained after removing overnight returns; and Sample 3 denotes sample obtained after removing first and last 30-minutes]

4.2 RETURNS RELATIONSHIP BETWEEN SPOT AND FUTURES MARKETS FOR INDIVIDUAL STOCKS

Derivatives' trading is more than a decade old phenomenon in the Indian capital market. Almost all of the studies which have investigated the issue of lead-lag relationship between spot and futures markets have examined the behavior of stock indices only. Only a few studies have investigated the matter of price discovery at the level of individual stocks. Some of the reason for this may be low trading activity in the futures contracts of individual stocks or absence of futures contracts altogether. But in the recent years, trading volume in derivatives contracts of individual stocks has also surpassed the trading volume in the spot market by many folds. Therefore, it is important to examine relationships between futures and spot markets for individual stocks also. Further, analysis of individual stocks would reveal whether futures and spot relationship for CNX Nifty and its associated futures contract is also supported by its constituent stocks.

The following sub-sections describe the returns relationship between futures and spot markets of individual stocks.

4.2.1 Error Correction mechanism for Full Sample

First of all, all the 50 constituent stocks of CNX Nifty are subjected to Augmented Dickey-Fuller (ADF) test to determine whether the price series of the stocks are stationary or not. The results of the ADF test are summarized in Table 4A.1 in the appendix I. As expected, the price series of all the 50 stocks for spot as well as futures markets have a unit root in their levels and are therefore non-stationary. Table 4A.1 also reports the summary results of the ADF test applied on the first differences of the components stocks of CNX Nifty. The null hypothesis that the first differences i.e., returns have a unit root is rejected for all the 50 stocks. Therefore, it can be concluded that all the 50 stocks are integrated of the order 1, i.e., I(1).

After confirming that all the underlying time series are integrated of order one, the next step is to test whether the spot and futures series for the underlying stocks are cointegrated. For this purpose Johansen-Juselius (1990) procedure has been utilized. The results of J-J cointegration analysis are shown in Table 4A.2 in the appendix I. The table reports the results of two likelihood ratio test statistics namely trace and maximum eigenvalue test. The results of both the test statistics reveal that futures and spot price series for each of the fifty stocks are cointegrated.

Once it is found that the two time series are cointegrated, then the appropriate modeling strategy is to estimate an Error Correction Model (ECM). For each of the 50 stocks, the following specification of VECM given below is estimated:

$$\Delta S_t = \phi_s + \alpha_s ect_{t-1} + \sum_{i=1}^{k} \alpha_i \Delta S_{t-i} + \sum_{i=1}^{k} \beta_i \Delta F_{t-i} + \varepsilon_{s,t} \quad \ldots\ldots\ldots (4.1a)$$

$$\Delta F_t = \phi_f + \alpha_f ect_{t-1} + \sum_{i=1}^{k} \gamma_i \Delta S_{t-i} + \sum_{i=1}^{k} \delta_i \Delta F_{t-i} + \varepsilon_{f,t} \quad \ldots\ldots\ldots (4.2b)$$

Where,

$\Delta S_t = S_t - S_{t-1}$ i.e., first difference of log of spot prices

$\Delta F_t = F_t - F_{t-1}$ i.e., first difference of log of futures prices

ect_{t-1} = lagged residual term from potentially cointegrating regression, $S_t = \alpha_s + \beta F_t + ect_t$

ϕ_s, ϕ_f = constants

α_s, α_f = coefficient of the error correction term

α_i, β_i, γ_i and δ_i = coefficients of lagged terms

$\varepsilon_{s,t}$, $\varepsilon_{f,t}$ = residual term at time t

Table 4.10 presents coefficients of the error correction term based on eqs. 4.1a and 4.1b along with standard errors and p-values. From the table, it can be seen that out of fifty stocks, the following fifteen stocks have significant α_s, i.e., coefficient of the error correction term (ect_{t-1}) for the spot market at 5% or 10% level of significance:

- ACC— significant at 5% level

- AMBUJACEM— significant at 5% level

- BHEL— significant at 5% level

- BPCL— significant at 5% level

- CIPLA— significant at 5% level

- HDFC— significant at 5% level

- HINDUNILVR— significant at 5% level

- JINDALSTEL— significant at 5% level

- MARUTI— significant at 5% level

- NTPC— significant at 5% level

- POWERGRID— significant at 5% level

- RCOM— significant at 10% level

- SAIL— significant at 10% level

- SIEMENS— significant at 10% level

- TATAMOTORS— significant at 10% level

The following twenty-two stocks have significant α_f, i.e., coefficient of the error correction term (ect_{t-1}) for the futures market:

- AXISBANK— significant at 5% level

- BAJAJAUTO— significant at 5% level

- BHARTIARTL— significant at 5% level

- BHEL— significant at 10% level

- BPCL— significant at 5% level

- DLF— significant at 10% level

- DRREDDY— significant at 10% level

- GAIL— significant at 5% level

- GRASIM— significant at 5% level

- HCLTECH— significant at 5% level

- HDFCBANK— significant at 10% level

- HEROMOTOCO— significant at 5% level

- ICICIBANK— significant at 5% level

- ITC— significant at 5% level

- JPASSOCIAT— significant at 5% level

- KOTAKBANK— significant at 5% level

- LT— significant at 5% level

- SIEMENS— significant at 5% level

- STER— significant at 5% level

- SUNPHARMA— significant at 5% level

- TATAPOWER— significant at 5% level

- TCS— significant at 5% level

For full sample period, 37 out of 50 stocks have significant error correction term, ect_{t-1}. 15 stocks have significant error correction term (ect_{t-1}) for ΔS_t and 22 stocks have significant error correction term for ΔF_t. Further, 3 stocks viz., BHEL, BPCL and SIEMENS have significant error correction term for both spot and futures markets.

Table 4.10: Coefficients of Error Correction Term (ECT) for full sample-

Company	ΔS_t			ΔF_t		
	ect_{t-1}	Std. Error	p-value	ect_{t-1}	Std. Error	p-value
ACC	-0.0112**	0.0036	0.0018	0	0.0036	0.9928
AMBUJACEM	-0.0084**	0.0034	0.0132	0.0034	0.0032	0.2961
AXISBANK	0.0031	0.0027	0.2436	0.0069**	0.0027	0.0098
BAJAJAUTO	-0.0039	0.0038	0.2988	0.0086**	0.0037	0.0201
BHARTIARTL	-0.0003	0.0077	0.9721	0.0187**	0.0076	0.0144
BHEL	-0.0183**	0.0038	0.0000	-0.007*	0.0038	0.0704
BPCL	-0.0582**	0.0142	0.0000	-0.0395**	0.0140	0.0047
CAIRN	-0.0034	0.0033	0.3054	0.0051	0.0032	0.1151
CIPLA	-0.0129**	0.0057	0.0231	0.0088	0.0056	0.1199
COALINDIA	-0.003	0.0021	0.1600	0.0017	0.0021	0.4113
DLF	0.0014	0.0055	0.7991	0.0105*	0.0055	0.0539
DRREDDY	-0.0055	0.0040	0.1701	0.0076*	0.0040	0.0586
GAIL	-0.0003	0.0037	0.9436	0.0111**	0.0036	0.0024
GRASIM	-0.0053	0.0039	0.1766	0.0131**	0.0040	0.0011
HCLTECH	-0.0032	0.0049	0.5125	0.0125**	0.0047	0.0081
HDFC	-0.0082**	0.0031	0.0072	-0.0017	0.0029	0.5636
HDFCBANK	-0.0037	0.0036	0.3047	0.0063*	0.0036	0.0767
HEROMOTOCO	-0.0008	0.0021	0.7191	0.0044**	0.0021	0.0371
HINDALCO	-0.0077	0.0104	0.4602	0.0127	0.0105	0.2266
HINDUNILVR	-0.0159**	0.0048	0.0008	-0.0046	0.0046	0.3166
ICICIBANK	0.002	0.0026	0.4476	0.0051**	0.0026	0.0499
IDFC	-0.0014	0.0036	0.6968	0.0042	0.0036	0.2395
INFY	-0.0033	0.0042	0.4330	0.0014	0.0042	0.7384
ITC	0.0028	0.0027	0.3169	0.009**	0.0027	0.0009
JINDALSTEL	-0.0148*	0.0082	0.0704	0.0108	0.0082	0.1885
JPASSOCIAT	0.006	0.0044	0.1660	0.0128**	0.0044	0.0038
KOTAKBANK	0.0013	0.0051	0.7962	0.0222**	0.0049	0.0000
LT	0.002	0.0048	0.6847	0.0116**	0.0049	0.0175
M&M	-0.0029	0.0038	0.4461	0.0059	0.0037	0.1113
MARUTI	-0.0109*	0.0056	0.0506	0.0032	0.0055	0.5605

NTPC	-0.0068**	0.0033	0.0376	0.0043	0.0032	0.1789
ONGC	-0.0035	0.0029	0.2336	0.0016	0.0029	0.5739
PNB	-0.0017	0.0026	0.5110	0.0027	0.0027	0.3134
POWERGRID	-0.0106**	0.0040	0.0083	0.0063	0.0040	0.1082
RANBAXY	-0.0104	0.0063	0.1008	0.0098	0.0064	0.1216
RCOM	-0.0175*	0.0099	0.0765	0.0068	0.0101	0.5006
RELIANCE	-0.0029	0.0041	0.4829	0.0051	0.0041	0.2176
RELINFRA	-0.0052	0.0055	0.3381	0.004	0.0056	0.4775
RPOWER	-0.0077	0.0060	0.2002	0.008	0.0063	0.1993
SAIL	-0.0156**	0.0040	0.0001	-0.0025	0.0042	0.5531
SBIN	-0.0029	0.0027	0.2839	0.0011	0.0028	0.6917
SESAGOA	-0.0026	0.0026	0.3174	0.0029	0.0026	0.2601
SIEMENS	-0.0169**	0.0069	0.0142	0.0207**	0.0069	0.0027
STER	-0.0023	0.0047	0.6234	0.0089*	0.0048	0.0614
SUNPHARMA	0.0001	0.0050	0.9784	0.0194**	0.0049	0.0001
TATAMOTORS	-0.0086*	0.0049	0.0789	-0.0022	0.0049	0.6516
TATAPOWER	-0.0031	0.0043	0.4716	0.0107**	0.0044	0.0144
TATASTEEL	-0.0018	0.0022	0.4140	0.0015	0.0022	0.4897
TCS	0.0004	0.0036	0.9122	0.0089**	0.0036	0.0127
WIPRO	-0.0037	0.0044	0.4050	0.0067	0.0044	0.1277

[Notes: ** and * denotes significance at 5% an 10% level respectively]

Cointegration relationship for each of the 50 individual stocks has also been examined by using the following specification of VECM:

$$\Delta S_t = \phi_s + \alpha_s z_{t-1} + \sum_{i=1}^{k} \alpha_i \Delta S_{t-i} + \sum_{i=1}^{k} \beta_i \Delta F_{t-i} + \varepsilon_{s,t} \quad \ldots\ldots\ldots (4.2a)$$

$$\Delta F_t = \phi_f + \alpha_f z_{t-1} + \sum_{i=1}^{k} \gamma_i \Delta S_{t-i} + \sum_{i=1}^{k} \delta_i \Delta F_{t-i} + \varepsilon_{f,t} \quad \ldots\ldots\ldots (4.2b)$$

Where,

z_{t-1} = lagged basis term given by: $F_{t-1} - S_{t-1}$

All other variables/coefficients are defined as in eqs. 4.1a and 4.1b.

Table 4.11 summarizes the results of VECM based on eqs. 4.2a and 4.2b. The table presents the coefficient of the error correction term (z_{t-1}) for full sample period. From the table it can be seen that α_s is significant for 13 stocks while α_f is significant for 26

stocks. Further, for 5 stocks viz., BPCL, CIPLA, LT, POWERGRID and SIEMENS

both α_s and α_f are significant. This implies that for these 5 stocks both spot and futures

markets respond to correct for disequilibrium from the long-term relationship.

Table 4.11: Coefficients of z_{t-1} for full sample-

Company	ΔS_t			ΔF_t		
	z_{t-1}	Std. Error	p-value	z_{t-1}	Std. Error	p-value
ACC	0.0071**	0.0033	0.0314	-0.0027	0.0033	0.4157
AMBUJACEM	0.0033	0.0030	0.2815	-0.0071**	0.0029	0.0140
AXISBANK	-0.004	0.0026	0.1222	-0.0075**	0.0026	0.0033
BAJAJAUTO	0.0018	0.0036	0.6141	-0.0097**	0.0036	0.0063
BHARTIARTL	-0.0004	0.0077	0.9595	-0.0193**	0.0076	0.0116
BHEL	0.0168**	0.0038	0.0000	0.0055	0.0038	0.1448
BPCL	0.0622**	0.0135	0.0000	0.0457**	0.0133	0.0006
CAIRN	0.0038	0.0033	0.2495	-0.0046	0.0032	0.1472
CIPLA	0.0111**	0.0057	0.0488	-0.0103*	0.0056	0.0668
COALINDIA	0.0013	0.0020	0.5099	-0.0026	0.0019	0.1688
DLF	-0.0021	0.0055	0.7010	-0.0112**	0.0055	0.0402
DRREDDY	0.0046	0.0039	0.2390	-0.008**	0.0040	0.0437
GAIL	-0.0004	0.0037	0.9136	-0.0115**	0.0036	0.0014
GRASIM	0.0017	0.0037	0.6497	-0.0148**	0.0038	0.0001
HCLTECH	0.0031	0.0049	0.5244	-0.0126**	0.0047	0.0075
HDFC	0.0044*	0.0026	0.0899	-0.0008	0.0025	0.7424
HDFCBANK	-0.0015	0.0032	0.6402	-0.0094**	0.0031	0.0025
HEROMOTOCO	0.001	0.0021	0.6274	-0.0041*	0.0021	0.0515
HINDALCO	0.0017	0.0098	0.8639	-0.0166*	0.0099	0.0942
HINDUNILVR	0.0153**	0.0047	0.0012	0.0041	0.0046	0.3713
ICICIBANK	-0.0009	0.0026	0.7187	-0.004	0.0026	0.1175
IDFC	-0.0026	0.0031	0.4089	-0.0067**	0.0031	0.0301
INFY	0.0018	0.0041	0.6667	-0.0027	0.0041	0.5031
ITC	-0.0036	0.0027	0.1804	-0.0096**	0.0026	0.0003
JINDALSTEL	0.0139*	0.0081	0.0849	-0.011	0.0081	0.1703
JPASSOCIAT	-0.0049	0.0043	0.2593	-0.0115**	0.0044	0.0086
KOTAKBANK	-0.0014	0.0051	0.7821	-0.0222**	0.0049	0.0000
LT	-0.0075*	0.0043	0.0823	-0.0151**	0.0044	0.0006
M&M	0.0004	0.0036	0.9069	-0.0076**	0.0036	0.0314
MARUTI	0.0061	0.0051	0.2284	-0.0054	0.0050	0.2811
NTPC	0.0058*	0.0032	0.0758	-0.0051	0.0032	0.1074
ONGC	0.0027	0.0029	0.3580	-0.0023	0.0028	0.4128
PNB	0.0007	0.0026	0.7936	-0.0036	0.0026	0.1703

POWERGRID	0.0084**	0.0039	0.0336	-0.008**	0.0039	0.0402
RANBAXY	0.0097	0.0062	0.1158	-0.0098	0.0062	0.1131
RCOM	0.0173*	0.0099	0.0784	-0.007	0.0101	0.4879
RELIANCE	0.0029	0.0041	0.4734	-0.005	0.0041	0.2203
RELINFRA	0.0053	0.0055	0.3354	-0.0039	0.0056	0.4810
RPOWER	0.0077	0.0060	0.1992	-0.0081	0.0063	0.1970
SAIL	0.0157**	0.0040	0.0001	0.0025	0.0042	0.5520
SBIN	0.0032	0.0027	0.2450	-0.0008	0.0028	0.7687
SESAGOA	0.0024	0.0026	0.3599	-0.0032	0.0026	0.2239
SIEMENS	0.0159**	0.0068	0.0203	-0.0214**	0.0069	0.0019
STER	0.0003	0.0046	0.9554	-0.0107**	0.0047	0.0220
SUNPHARMA	0.0001	0.0050	0.9843	-0.0192**	0.0049	0.0001
TATAMOTORS	0.0063	0.0047	0.1820	0.0003	0.0047	0.9426
TATAPOWER	0.0009	0.0042	0.8377	-0.0122**	0.0042	0.0039
TATASTEEL	0.0018	0.0022	0.4136	-0.0014	0.0022	0.5291
TCS	0.0001	0.0036	0.9878	-0.0083**	0.0035	0.0187
WIPRO	0.0048	0.0044	0.2730	-0.0054	0.0043	0.2097

[Notes: ** and * denotes significance at 5% an 10% level respectively]

4.2.2 Error correction mechanism after removing overnight returns

The issue regarding whether spot or futures market responds to correct for disequilibrium from long-term relationship has also been examined after removing overnight returns. Table 4.12 shows the coefficients of error correction term from the VECM based on eqs. 4.1a and 4.1b. It can be seen from the table that 27 out of 50 stocks have significant error correction term. Further, 19 stocks have significant error correction term at 5% level and 8 stocks have significant error correction term at 10% level of significance. α_s, i.e., the coefficient of the error correction term for spot market is significant for 8 stocks while α_f, the coefficient of error correction term for futures market is significant for 23 stocks. In addition, there are 4 stocks for which both α_s and α_f are significant.

Table 4.13 reports estimates of α_s and α_f along with standard errors and p-values based on specification given in eqs. 4.2a and 4.2b. It is found that 35 out of 50 stocks have significant α_s or α_f. α_s is significant for 8 stocks and α_f is significant for 32 stocks. Besides for 5 stocks, both α_s and α_f are significant.

Table 4.12: Coefficients of Error Correction Term (ECT) for sample after removing overnight returns-

Company	ΔS_t			ΔF_t		
	ect_{t-1}	Std. Error	p-value	ect_{t-1}	Std. Error	p-value
ACC	-0.0047	0.0033	0.1521	0.0008	0.0033	0.8107
AMBUJACEM	-0.0005	0.0031	0.8705	0.0049	0.0030	0.1060
AXISBANK	0.0051**	0.0024	0.0301	0.0064**	0.0024	0.0068
BAJAJAUTO	0.0006	0.0034	0.8531	0.0062*	0.0034	0.0693
BHARTIARTL	0.0035	0.0068	0.6097	0.0143**	0.0068	0.0348
BHEL	-0.0118**	0.0034	0.0006	-0.005	0.0035	0.1475
BPCL	-0.0014	0.0049	0.7684	0.0095**	0.0048	0.0486
CAIRN	0.0012	0.0028	0.6647	0.007**	0.0027	0.0095
CIPLA	-0.0035	0.0049	0.4813	0.0059	0.0049	0.2284
COALINDIA	0.0004	0.0019	0.8257	0.0027	0.0019	0.1441
DLF	0.0081	0.0050	0.1029	0.0109**	0.0050	0.0307
DRREDDY	-0.0025	0.0035	0.4722	0.0057	0.0035	0.1048
GAIL	0.0021	0.0034	0.5416	0.0113**	0.0033	0.0007
GRASIM	-0.0032	0.0036	0.3755	0.0132**	0.0036	0.0003
HCLTECH	-0.0029	0.0042	0.4894	0.0073*	0.0041	0.0742
HDFC	-0.0044*	0.0027	0.0999	-0.0015	0.0025	0.5498
HDFCBANK	-0.0022	0.0033	0.5093	0.0041	0.0032	0.2014
HEROMOTOCO	0.0011	0.0019	0.5593	0.0038**	0.0019	0.0426
HINDALCO	-0.0048	0.0068	0.4788	0.0075	0.0070	0.2812
HINDUNILVR	-0.0043	0.0034	0.2086	-0.0006	0.0033	0.8640
ICICIBANK	0.0036*	0.0022	0.0998	0.0044**	0.0022	0.0484
IDFC	0.0008	0.0033	0.8089	0.003	0.0033	0.3688
INFY	0.0001	0.0023	0.9674	0.003	0.0023	0.2032
ITC	0.0055**	0.0024	0.0250	0.0078**	0.0024	0.0012
JINDALSTEL	-0.0098	0.0075	0.1889	0.0043	0.0075	0.5616
JPASSOCIAT	0.0051	0.0038	0.1834	0.0085**	0.0039	0.0290
KOTAKBANK	0.0058	0.0047	0.2174	0.0226**	0.0047	0.0000
LT	0.0045	0.0043	0.2957	0.0079*	0.0044	0.0702
M&M	0.0012	0.0035	0.7275	0.0066*	0.0034	0.0516
MARUTI	-0.0009	0.0048	0.8500	0.0085*	0.0048	0.0740
NTPC	-0.0022	0.0030	0.4673	0.005*	0.0029	0.0875
ONGC	-0.0019	0.0025	0.4387	0.0018	0.0025	0.4666
PNB	0.0012	0.0024	0.6163	0.0022	0.0024	0.3600
POWERGRID	-0.0091**	0.0037	0.0145	0.0017	0.0036	0.6424

RANBAXY	-0.0057	0.0057	0.3168	0.0061	0.0057	0.2851
RCOM	-0.012	0.0093	0.1958	0.0036	0.0096	0.7107
RELIANCE	-0.0005	0.0036	0.8783	0.0021	0.0036	0.5688
RELINFRA	-0.0042	0.0050	0.3973	0.0004	0.0052	0.9333
RPOWER	-0.0022	0.0056	0.6988	0.0062	0.0059	0.2927
SAIL	-0.0077**	0.0038	0.0402	-0.0031	0.0039	0.4335
SBIN	-0.0016	0.0024	0.5033	0.0002	0.0025	0.9300
SESAGOA	-0.0026	0.0023	0.2703	0.0017	0.0023	0.4564
SIEMENS	-0.0173**	0.0064	0.0066	0.0206**	0.0064	0.0014
STER	-0.0013	0.0041	0.7503	0.0053	0.0042	0.2092
SUNPHARMA	0.0051	0.0044	0.2464	0.0175**	0.0044	0.0001
TATAMOTORS	-0.0044	0.0039	0.2601	-0.0018	0.0040	0.6573
TATAPOWER	-0.0005	0.0038	0.8843	0.0084**	0.0039	0.0297
TATASTEEL	-0.0001	0.0019	0.9405	0.001	0.0019	0.6049
TCS	0.0016	0.0032	0.6199	0.0064**	0.0031	0.0405
WIPRO	-0.0005	0.0035	0.8804	0.0059*	0.0035	0.0906

[Notes: ** and * denotes significance at 5% an 10% level respectively]

Table 4.13: Coefficients of z_{t-1} for sample after removing overnight returns-

Company	zt-1	Std. Error	p-value	zt-1	Std. Error	p-value
ACC	0.0013	0.0030	0.6653	-0.0053*	0.0030	0.0790
AMBUJACEM	-0.0042	0.0028	0.1306	-0.0102**	0.0027	0.0001
AXISBANK	-0.0046**	0.0023	0.0426	-0.0061**	0.0023	0.0070
BAJAJAUTO	-0.0024	0.0033	0.4634	-0.0095**	0.0033	0.0041
BHARTIARTL	-0.006	0.0068	0.3756	-0.0197**	0.0068	0.0037
BHEL	0.0122**	0.0034	0.0003	0.0043	0.0034	0.2059
BPCL	0	0.0046	0.9973	-0.0132**	0.0046	0.0040
CAIRN	0.0025	0.0027	0.3553	-0.0061**	0.0027	0.0227
CIPLA	0.0019	0.0049	0.6936	-0.0125**	0.0049	0.0105
COALINDIA	-0.0006	0.0017	0.7438	-0.003*	0.0017	0.0802
DLF	-0.0087*	0.0050	0.0780	-0.013**	0.0050	0.0103
DRREDDY	0.0016	0.0034	0.6300	-0.0077**	0.0034	0.0243
GAIL	-0.0019	0.0033	0.5605	-0.0146**	0.0033	0.0000
GRASIM	0.0005	0.0034	0.8741	-0.0187**	0.0035	0.0000
HCLTECH	0.0029	0.0042	0.4953	-0.011**	0.0041	0.0070
HDFC	0.0026	0.0023	0.2599	-0.0011	0.0022	0.6263
HDFCBANK	-0.0004	0.0029	0.8772	-0.0069**	0.0028	0.0146
HEROMOTOCO	-0.0007	0.0018	0.7211	-0.004**	0.0019	0.0318
HINDALCO	0.0031	0.0064	0.6295	-0.0114*	0.0066	0.0847
HINDUNILVR	0.0046	0.0034	0.1767	-0.0008	0.0033	0.8057
ICICIBANK	-0.0031	0.0022	0.1541	-0.0042*	0.0022	0.0599
IDFC	-0.0033	0.0028	0.2482	-0.0048*	0.0029	0.0935

INFY	0.0005	0.0023	0.8233	-0.0028	0.0023	0.2201
ITC	-0.0054**	0.0024	0.0223	-0.009**	0.0023	0.0001
JINDALSTEL	0.0118	0.0073	0.1094	-0.0071	0.0074	0.3313
JPASSOCIAT	-0.004	0.0038	0.2887	-0.0086**	0.0038	0.0255
KOTAKBANK	-0.0045	0.0047	0.3421	-0.025**	0.0047	0.0000
LT	-0.0081**	0.0039	0.0345	-0.0122**	0.0039	0.0018
M&M	-0.0017	0.0033	0.5990	-0.0087**	0.0032	0.0072
MARUTI	-0.0024	0.0044	0.5845	-0.0117**	0.0044	0.0076
NTPC	0.0022	0.0030	0.4652	-0.0066**	0.0029	0.0230
ONGC	0.0014	0.0025	0.5613	-0.0027	0.0024	0.2589
PNB	-0.0017	0.0023	0.4649	-0.0036	0.0024	0.1301
POWERGRID	0.008**	0.0037	0.0291	-0.0045	0.0036	0.2102
RANBAXY	0.0063	0.0055	0.2568	-0.0087	0.0056	0.1227
RCOM	0.013	0.0093	0.1600	-0.0091	0.0096	0.3439
RELIANCE	0.0005	0.0036	0.8843	-0.0034	0.0036	0.3385
RELINFRA	0.0051	0.0050	0.3102	-0.0011	0.0052	0.8264
RPOWER	0.0028	0.0056	0.6248	-0.009	0.0059	0.1277
SAIL	0.0079**	0.0038	0.0351	0.0009	0.0039	0.8156
SBIN	0.0017	0.0024	0.4698	-0.0005	0.0025	0.8446
SESAGOA	0.0029	0.0023	0.2102	-0.0022	0.0023	0.3422
SIEMENS	0.0181**	0.0063	0.0042	-0.0302**	0.0064	0.0000
STER	0.0007	0.0041	0.8712	-0.0075*	0.0041	0.0698
SUNPHARMA	-0.0066	0.0044	0.1368	-0.0223**	0.0044	0.0000
TATAMOTORS	0.0039	0.0038	0.3134	0.0003	0.0039	0.9327
TATAPOWER	-0.0001	0.0036	0.9684	-0.0117**	0.0037	0.0017
TATASTEEL	0	0.0018	0.9988	-0.0017	0.0019	0.3819
TCS	-0.0023	0.0032	0.4616	-0.0084**	0.0031	0.0071
WIPRO	0.0002	0.0034	0.9457	-0.0078**	0.0034	0.0232

[Notes: ** and * denotes significance at 5% an 10% level respectively]

4.2.3 Error correction mechanism after removing first and last thirty minutes

It is usually observed that first and last thirty minutes of a trading day have more than average trading activity and excessive volatility. The behavior of spot and futures markets may be disturbed by excessive trading and accompanying volatility during this time. Therefore, the error correction mechanism between spot and futures markets has also been examined after removing first and last thirty minutes of a trading day. Table 4.14 presents estimates of error correction term for eqs. 4.1a and 4.1b. It is observed from the table that 11 stocks have significant α_s and 23 stocks have significant α_f. Further, for 7 stocks both α_s and α_f are significant.

Table 4.15 reports the coefficients of the error correction term based on specification presented in eqs. 4.2a and 4.2b. It can be seen from the table that α_s is significant for 11 stocks and α_f is significant for 27 stocks. 9 stocks have significant α_s as well as α_f.

Table 4.14: Coefficients of Error Correction Term (ECT) removing first and last 30 minutes-

Company	ΔS_t			ΔF_t		
	ect_{t-1}	Std. Error	p-value	ect_{t-1}	Std. Error	p-value
ACC	-0.0078**	0.0033	0.0181	-0.0009	0.0034	0.7941
AMBUJACEM	0.0013	0.0031	0.6688	0.0059*	0.0030	0.0529
AXISBANK	0.0047*	0.0024	0.0511	0.0055**	0.0025	0.0248
BAJAJAUTO	0.0019	0.0034	0.5760	0.0053	0.0034	0.1253
BHARTIARTL	0.0101	0.0067	0.1287	0.0179**	0.0067	0.0079
BHEL	-0.0102**	0.0035	0.0032	-0.0036	0.0036	0.3128
BPCL	0.0047	0.0049	0.3358	0.0128**	0.0049	0.0087
CAIRN	0.0035	0.0027	0.1935	0.0072**	0.0027	0.0079
CIPLA	-0.0008	0.0049	0.8710	0.0035	0.0049	0.4765
COALINDIA	0.0034*	0.0018	0.0631	0.0043**	0.0018	0.0194
DLF	0.0082	0.0052	0.1113	0.0116**	0.0053	0.0288
DRREDDY	0.0015	0.0034	0.6680	0.0062*	0.0035	0.0727
GAIL	0.0038	0.0032	0.2325	0.0117**	0.0032	0.0003
GRASIM	-0.0021	0.0035	0.5419	0.0082**	0.0036	0.0220
HCLTECH	0.0011	0.0041	0.7863	0.0108**	0.0041	0.0081
HDFC	-0.003	0.0025	0.2342	-0.0014	0.0025	0.5765
HDFCBANK	0.0005	0.0033	0.8747	0.0041	0.0033	0.2169
HEROMOTOCO	0.0024	0.0018	0.1890	0.005**	0.0019	0.0079
HINDALCO	0.0008	0.0070	0.9092	0.0105	0.0073	0.1520
HINDUNILVR	-0.0017	0.0032	0.5999	-0.001	0.0032	0.7461
ICICIBANK	0.0032	0.0023	0.1653	0.0032	0.0023	0.1666
IDFC	0.0003	0.0033	0.9327	0.0012	0.0034	0.7342
INFY	0.0009	0.0023	0.7037	0.0023	0.0023	0.3231
ITC	0.0045*	0.0024	0.0652	0.0044*	0.0024	0.0702
JINDALSTEL	-0.0146*	0.0075	0.0509	0.001	0.0076	0.8972
JPASSOCIAT	0.0048	0.0039	0.2184	0.0086**	0.0040	0.0319
KOTAKBANK	0.0092*	0.0049	0.0601	0.0194**	0.0049	0.0001
LT	0.0089**	0.0045	0.0461	0.0114**	0.0046	0.0125

M&M	0.0031	0.0034	0.3633	0.007**	0.0034	0.0386
MARUTI	0.0033	0.0047	0.4883	0.0086*	0.0048	0.0718
NTPC	-0.0018	0.0029	0.5309	0.0031	0.0030	0.2901
ONGC	-0.0004	0.0024	0.8799	0.0027	0.0024	0.2678
PNB	0.0007	0.0025	0.7694	0.0001	0.0026	0.9838
POWERGRID	-0.006*	0.0036	0.0972	0.0021	0.0036	0.5615
RANBAXY	-0.0029	0.0057	0.6133	0.0076	0.0058	0.1924
RCOM	-0.0118	0.0097	0.2229	0.0005	0.0101	0.9617
RELIANCE	0.0023	0.0036	0.5124	0.0042	0.0037	0.2547
RELINFRA	-0.0051	0.0053	0.3292	-0.0014	0.0055	0.7941
RPOWER	-0.0016	0.0059	0.7901	0.0084	0.0062	0.1786
SAIL	-0.0057	0.0039	0.1487	-0.0016	0.0042	0.6918
SBIN	-0.0001	0.0026	0.9778	0.0011	0.0027	0.6731
SESAGOA	0.0002	0.0024	0.9258	0.0005	0.0024	0.8240
SIEMENS	-0.0033	0.0065	0.6091	0.0204**	0.0066	0.0019
STER	-0.0007	0.0042	0.8743	0.0053	0.0044	0.2246
SUNPHARMA	0.0082*	0.0043	0.0590	0.0152**	0.0044	0.0005
TATAMOTORS	-0.0025	0.0039	0.5329	-0.0013	0.0040	0.7453
TATAPOWER	0.003	0.0038	0.4199	0.0097**	0.0039	0.0133
TATASTEEL	-0.0004	0.0019	0.8189	0.0007	0.0020	0.7187
TCS	0.0055*	0.0030	0.0706	0.0068**	0.0031	0.0270
WIPRO	0.0041	0.0033	0.2142	0.0085**	0.0033	0.0113

[Notes: ** and * denotes significance at 5% an 10% level respectively]

Table 4.15: Coefficients of z_{t-1} after removing first and last 30 minutes-

Company	ΔS_t			ΔF_t		
	z_{t-1}	Std. Error	p-value	z_{t-1}	Std. Error	p-value
ACC	0.0022	0.0030	0.4717	-0.0033	0.0031	0.2829
AMBUJACEM	-0.0069**	0.0027	0.0120	-0.0113**	0.0027	0.0000
AXISBANK	-0.0049**	0.0023	0.0335	-0.0058**	0.0024	0.0140
BAJAJAUTO	-0.004	0.0033	0.2157	-0.007**	0.0033	0.0352
BHARTIARTL	-0.0118*	0.0067	0.0761	-0.0207**	0.0067	0.0022
BHEL	0.0098**	0.0034	0.0042	0.0027	0.0035	0.4425
BPCL	-0.0043	0.0047	0.3580	-0.0137**	0.0046	0.0032
CAIRN	-0.0026	0.0027	0.3245	-0.0069**	0.0027	0.0103
CIPLA	0.001	0.0049	0.8425	-0.0061	0.0049	0.2121
COALINDIA	-0.0037**	0.0017	0.0273	-0.0043**	0.0017	0.0112
DLF	-0.009*	0.0051	0.0798	-0.0127**	0.0053	0.0162
. DRREDDY	-0.0032	0.0033	0.3306	-0.0076**	0.0034	0.0245
GAIL	-0.004	0.0032	0.2109	-0.0125**	0.0032	0.0001
GRASIM	0	0.0033	0.9964	-0.0106**	0.0034	0.0019
HCLTECH	-0.0015	0.0041	0.7181	-0.0124**	0.0041	0.0022

HDFC	-0.0005	0.0022	0.8078	-0.0006	0.0021	0.7759
HDFCBANK	-0.0031	0.0029	0.2886	-0.0061**	0.0029	0.0341
HEROMOTOCO	-0.0017	0.0018	0.3459	-0.0047**	0.0019	0.0108
HINDALCO	-0.0026	0.0067	0.7004	-0.0124*	0.0069	0.0725
HINDUNILVR	0.0017	0.0032	0.5925	0.0007	0.0032	0.8307
ICICIBANK	-0.0029	0.0023	0.2046	-0.003	0.0023	0.1915
IDFC	-0.0037	0.0029	0.2068	-0.0035	0.0029	0.2291
INFY	-0.001	0.0022	0.6648	-0.0025	0.0023	0.2746
ITC	-0.0044*	0.0023	0.0635	-0.0048**	0.0024	0.0427
JINDALSTEL	0.0162**	0.0074	0.0277	-0.0003	0.0075	0.9697
JPASSOCIAT	-0.0035	0.0039	0.3584	-0.0079**	0.0040	0.0460
KOTAKBANK	-0.0079	0.0049	0.1067	-0.0193**	0.0049	0.0001
LT	-0.0139**	0.0040	0.0005	-0.0152**	0.0041	0.0002
M&M	-0.004	0.0032	0.2166	-0.0078**	0.0032	0.0163
MARUTI	-0.0068	0.0043	0.1140	-0.0113**	0.0044	0.0095
NTPC	0.002	0.0029	0.4860	-0.0031	0.0029	0.2977
ONGC	-0.0004	0.0024	0.8787	-0.0036	0.0024	0.1329
PNB	-0.0017	0.0024	0.4870	-0.0012	0.0025	0.6374
POWERGRID	0.0047	0.0036	0.1839	-0.003	0.0035	0.3875
RANBAXY	0.0008	0.0055	0.8845	-0.0104*	0.0057	0.0666
RCOM	0.0108	0.0097	0.2664	-0.0034	0.0101	0.7330
RELIANCE	-0.0027	0.0036	0.4577	-0.0047	0.0037	0.2017
RELINFRA	0.0051	0.0053	0.3348	0.0005	0.0055	0.9202
RPOWER	0.0012	0.0059	0.8403	-0.0097	0.0062	0.1196
SAIL	0.006	0.0039	0.1268	0.0014	0.0042	0.7300
SBIN	0.0004	0.0025	0.8777	-0.0009	0.0027	0.7419
SESAGOA	-0.0004	0.0024	0.8768	-0.0009	0.0024	0.7111
SIEMENS	0.0067	0.0065	0.3016	-0.0219**	0.0066	0.0008
STER	-0.0007	0.0041	0.8608	-0.0068	0.0043	0.1087
SUNPHARMA	-0.0079*	0.0043	0.0648	-0.016**	0.0043	0.0002
TATAMOTORS	0.0018	0.0038	0.6387	0.0006	0.0039	0.8857
TATAPOWER	-0.0035	0.0037	0.3394	-0.0101**	0.0038	0.0078
TATASTEEL	0.0001	0.0019	0.9648	-0.0012	0.0020	0.5348
TCS	-0.0054*	0.0030	0.0727	-0.0072**	0.0031	0.0189
WIPRO	-0.0034	0.0032	0.2856	-0.0089**	0.0033	0.0069

[Notes: ** and * denotes significance at 5% an 10% level respectively]

4.2.4 Lead-lag Relationship between spot and futures markets based on Granger Causality

To examine the direction of flow of information between spot and futures markets, Granger Causality test has been applied based on VAR. The results of Granger Causality test for full sample period (including overnight returns) are presented in Table 4.16. Table 4.17 shows the results of Granger Causality test for the restricted sample (after removing overnight returns). The results for both the full and the restricted sample are almost similar. It can be seen from the table that the null hypothesis that ΔS_t does not granger cause ΔF_t is rejected for all the 50 stocks. Similarly, the null hypothesis that ΔF_t does not granger cause ΔS_t is also rejected. This implies that past history of spot market returns is helpful in predicting returns from the futures market and vice versa. Thus, a feedback relationship exists between futures and spot markets for all the 50 constituent stocks. However, if we examine the size and significance of the lagged coefficients in the VAR model , then it appears that causality from futures to spot market is much stronger than in the reverse direction. Lead-lag relationship between spot and futures return series of individual stocks has also been examined after removing first and last 30-min data. BHARTIARTL is the only stock for which there is no granger causality from futures to spot market, otherwise for all other stocks there runs granger causality from spot to futures and futures to spot markets.

Table 4.16: Granger Causality Test for full sample-

Company	Spot does not Granger Cause Futures		Futures does not Granger Cause Spot	
	F-test	p-value	F-test	p-value
ACC	61.598**	0.0000	24.3606**	0.0000
AMBUJACEM	52.3226**	0.0000	30.2269**	0.0000
AXISBANK	24.1431**	0.0000	7.0089**	0.0000
BAJAJAUTO	68.4745**	0.0000	16.5669**	0.0000
BHARTIARTL	41.3765**	0.0000	2.7731**	0.0107
BHEL	27.0596**	0.0000	17.8809**	0.0000
BPCL	11.3285**	0.0000	3.2992**	0.0030
CAIRN	55.0877**	0.0000	23.1826**	0.0000
CIPLA	80.6303**	0.0000	18.4014**	0.0000
COALINDIA	79.8848**	0.0000	21.0517**	0.0000
DLF	14.2593**	0.0000	10.6763**	0.0000
DRREDDY	74.6449**	0.0000	20.219**	0.0000
GAIL	137.5067**	0.0000	8.8394**	0.0000
GRASIM	121.3113**	0.0000	59.9665**	0.0000
HCLTECH	81.8714**	0.0000	12.8117**	0.0000
HDFC	57.9784**	0.0000	25.0339**	0.0000
HDFCBANK	22.6819**	0.0000	20.3783**	0.0000
HEROMOTOCO	38.1385**	0.0000	30.0657**	0.0000
HINDALCO	24.4271**	0.0000	9.3114**	0.0000
HINDUNILVR	20.496**	0.0000	23.371**	0.0000
ICICIBANK	14.445**	0.0000	14.4184**	0.0000
IDFC	46.2933**	0.0000	5.8613**	0.0000
INFY	35.6595**	0.0000	2.5627*	0.0529
ITC	36.7092**	0.0000	12.2994**	0.0000
JINDALSTEL	22.255**	0.0000	13.5209**	0.0000
JPASSOCIAT	24.055**	0.0000	12.9206**	0.0000
KOTAKBANK	42.1862**	0.0000	34.3366**	0.0000
LT	14.5112**	0.0000	9.1325**	0.0000
M&M	41.9627**	0.0000	20.7742**	0.0000
MARUTI	39.0868**	0.0000	10.4755**	0.0000
NTPC	117.084**	0.0000	18.5292**	0.0000
ONGC	58.8536**	0.0000	11.5719**	0.0000
PNB	45.306**	0.0000	19.9521**	0.0000
POWERGRID	108.5538**	0.0000	27.2793**	0.0000
RANBAXY	39.6996**	0.0000	22.7684**	0.0000
RCOM	23.489**	0.0000	16.3771**	0.0000
RELIANCE	19.7071**	0.0000	16.786**	0.0000
RELINFRA	20.6449**	0.0000	11.6994**	0.0000
RPOWER	31.0015**	0.0000	27.0969**	0.0000
SAIL	72.1263**	0.0000	31.2901**	0.0000

SBIN	11.3433**	0.0000	7.9496**	0.0000
SESAGOA	37.2652**	0.0000	37.1285**	0.0000
SIEMENS	97.5313**	0.0000	44.4637**	0.0000
STER	46.6077**	0.0000	19.3367**	0.0000
SUNPHARMA	110.6392**	0.0000	14.0684**	0.0000
TATAMOTORS	26.112**	0.0000	6.244**	0.0001
TATAPOWER	93.0422**	0.0000	26.1755**	0.0000
TATASTEEL	21.3635**	0.0000	16.0505**	0.0000
TCS	35.5089**	0.0000	10.0585**	0.0000
WIPRO	59.6342**	0.0000	12.0184**	0.0000

[Notes: ** and * denotes significance at 5% an 10% level respectively]

Table 4.17: Granger Causality Test for Sample after removing overnight returns-

Company	Spot does not Granger Cause Futures		Futures does not Granger Cause Spot	
	F-test	p-value	F-test	p-value
ACC	68.012**	0.0000	24.3366**	0.0000
AMBUJACEM	84.7041**	0.0000	30.4528**	0.0000
AXISBANK	28.765**	0.0000	4.9119**	0.0006
BAJAJAUTO	67.4578**	0.0000	18.2684**	0.0000
BHARTIARTL	60.6412**	0.0000	4.5003**	0.0004
BHEL	51.2732**	0.0000	12.1337**	0.0000
BPCL	105.1609**	0.0000	16.5856**	0.0000
CAIRN	82.3427**	0.0000	5.9417**	0.0001
CIPLA	82.7474**	0.0000	18.897**	0.0000
COALINDIA	85.8854**	0.0000	10.4297**	0.0000
DLF	23.5182**	0.0000	11.9964**	0.0000
DRREDDY	99.4552**	0.0000	13.3708**	0.0000
GAIL	132.452**	0.0000	9.8742**	0.0000
GRASIM	122.2694**	0.0000	66.9137**	0.0000
HCLTECH	125.0405**	0.0000	7.2746**	0.0000
HDFC	56.052**	0.0000	20.528**	0.0000
HDFCBANK	40.5697**	0.0000	20.1993**	0.0000
HEROMOTOCO	59.3646**	0.0000	23.6857**	0.0000
HINDALCO	33.7886**	0.0000	21.7963**	0.0000
HINDUNILVR	46.7867**	0.0000	28.9613**	0.0000
ICICIBANK	17.9105**	0.0000	17.1341**	0.0000
IDFC	42.1867**	0.0000	9.3933**	0.0000
INFY	50.2163**	0.0000	17.8643**	0.0000
ITC	29.7189**	0.0000	21.5761**	0.0000
JINDALSTEL	28.5318**	0.0000	14.2618**	0.0000

JPASSOCIAT	26.2119**	0.0000	25.5685**	0.0000
KOTAKBANK	55.0421**	0.0000	43.1203**	0.0000
LT	30.3164**	0.0000	6.3338**	0.0000
M&M	45.7522**	0.0000	15.4377**	0.0000
MARUTI	60.8332**	0.0000	10.8211**	0.0000
NTPC	144.7251**	0.0000	15.6582**	0.0000
ONGC	88.0136**	0.0000	12.1355**	0.0000
PNB	43.9124**	0.0000	26.7994**	0.0000
POWERGRID	149.9015**	0.0000	19.073**	0.0000
RANBAXY	43.132**	0.0000	26.0088**	0.0000
RCOM	23.02**	0.0000	21.1808**	0.0000
RELIANCE	27.5295**	0.0000	10.0759**	0.0000
RELINFRA	17.2612**	0.0000	13.6296**	0.0000
RPOWER	30.4376**	0.0000	37.7534**	0.0000
SAIL	71.7931**	0.0000	37.838**	0.0000
SBIN	13.5122**	0.0000	9.6978**	0.0000
SESAGOA	47.9877**	0.0000	30.0356**	0.0000
SIEMENS	140.2072**	0.0000	49.0366**	0.0000
STER	54.9721**	0.0000	19.4998**	0.0000
SUNPHARMA	129.1385**	0.0000	14.5146**	0.0000
TATAMOTORS	28.7839**	0.0000	5.2303**	0.0003
TATAPOWER	134.5562**	0.0000	27.8867**	0.0000
TATASTEEL	26.0986**	0.0000	21.7794**	0.0000
TCS	62.9194**	0.0000	5.6571**	0.0002
WIPRO	95.8325**	0.0000	18.5056**	0.0000

[Notes: ** and * denotes significance at 5% an 10% level respectively]

Table 4.18: Granger Causality Test for Sample after removing first and last 30 minutes-

	Spot does not Granger Cause Futures		Futures does not Granger Cause Spot	
Company	F-test	p-value	F-test	p-value
ACC	64.3074**	0.0000	27.0747**	0.0000
AMBUJACEM	90.008**	0.0000	22.4602**	0.0000
AXISBANK	25.8526**	0.0000	5.9116**	0.0001
BAJAJAUTO	57.4061**	0.0000	15.2357**	0.0000
BHARTIARTL	76.3018**	0.0000	1.7174	0.1268
BHEL	42.1738**	0.0000	17.3365**	0.0000
BPCL	94.4267**	0.0000	15.7034**	0.0000
CAIRN	78.5149**	0.0000	12.7028**	0.0000
CIPLA	106.1664**	0.0000	15.1945**	0.0000
COALINDIA	115.9852**	0.0000	14.1293**	0.0000

DLF	16.6298**	0.0000	8.8122**	0.0000
DRREDDY	112.6789**	0.0000	15.0476**	0.0000
GAIL	172.5774**	0.0000	6.9375**	0.0000
GRASIM	145.0142**	0.0000	64.4158**	0.0000
HCLTECH	133.1391**	0.0000	3.6531**	0.0026
HDFC	49.9202**	0.0000	13.4933**	0.0000
HDFCBANK	23.5212**	0.0000	21**	0.0000
HEROMOTOCO	61.4315**	0.0000	21.799**	0.0000
HINDALCO	32.7785**	0.0000	27.3713**	0.0000
HINDUNILVR	41.1635**	0.0000	27.197**	0.0000
ICICIBANK	10.5902**	0.0000	13.3752**	0.0000
IDFC	43.523**	0.0000	10.6847**	0.0000
INFY	33.3864**	0.0000	18.9922**	0.0000
ITC	43.3201**	0.0000	18.2493**	0.0000
JINDALSTEL	32.4615**	0.0000	18.3927**	0.0000
JPASSOCIAT	20.2888**	0.0000	23.3649**	0.0000
KOTAKBANK	54.2198**	0.0000	33.9424**	0.0000
LT	30.9249**	0.0000	4.6928**	0.0003
M&M	50.4668**	0.0000	17.2842**	0.0000
MARUTI	55.7931**	0.0000	13.7276**	0.0000
NTPC	130.0904**	0.0000	15.7173**	0.0000
ONGC	77.2439**	0.0000	7.0129**	0.0000
PNB	30.8923**	0.0000	19.7625**	0.0000
POWERGRID	151.2435**	0.0000	16.114**	0.0000
RANBAXY	47.9723**	0.0000	22.7384**	0.0000
RCOM	14.2501**	0.0000	18.4451**	0.0000
RELIANCE	27.9233**	0.0000	9.7697**	0.0000
RELINFRA	16.8213**	0.0000	12.1826**	0.0000
RPOWER	29.2857**	0.0000	29.2035**	0.0000
SAIL	65.9561**	0.0000	32.063**	0.0000
SBIN	12.0986**	0.0000	10.1903**	0.0000
SESAGOA	38.1627**	0.0000	34.6549**	0.0000
SIEMENS	109.2336**	0.0000	31.0287**	0.0000
STER	57.8367**	0.0000	22.3873**	0.0000
SUNPHARMA	118.527**	0.0000	11.3314**	0.0000
TATAMOTORS	30.1922**	0.0000	4.0269**	0.0012
TATAPOWER	105.6559**	0.0000	20.2873**	0.0000
TATASTEEL	18.9564**	0.0000	14.3381**	0.0000
TCS	57.1324**	0.0000	6.909**	0.0000
WIPRO	120.2594**	0.0000	13.6236**	0.0000

[Notes: ** and * denotes significance at 5% an 10% level respectively]

4.3 CONCLUSION

This chapter has examined long-term and short-term relationships between futures and spot markets for CNX Nifty and all of its 50 constituent stocks. For examining the relationships 5-min transaction prices data has been used. For CNX Nifty, it has been found that futures and spot markets are cointegrated. It implies that though in the short-term the futures and the spot prices may deviate from each other, this deviation does not persist indefinitely implying that either the spot market or the futures responds/adjusts to correct for the disequilibrium. Further, for CNX Nifty, it is futures rather than the spot market which responds to restore the equilibrium. Similarly, each of the 50 stocks have been found to be cointegrated. For 41 out of 50 stocks error correction was taking place. There were 9 stocks for which neither spot nor futures market responds to correct the disequilibrium. Theoretically, for cointegration to exist at least one of the two series should have significant error correction term. The force behind this error correction is cost of carry which implies that if fairly large deviation exists between the two markets then arbitrage is possible. Insignificant error term may be due to two reasons. First, the deviation between the two markets is substantial to attract arbitrage but there is not sufficient liquidity in either the spot or the futures market so that arbitrageurs find it difficult to buy in one market and sell in other market simultaneously. Second, the error is not substantial which implies that though there is deviation between the two markets but this deviation is within the no arbitrage band.

The short-term relationships between futures and spot markets of CNX Nifty and each of its 50 constituent stocks have been examined buy employing Granger Causality test based on Vector Autoregressive Model (VAR). For the index as well as for all the 50 stocks, it has been found that both spot and futures markets granger causes each other implying that feedback relationship exists between the two markets.

Chapter-5
Empirical Evidence on Volatility Spillover between Futures and Spot Markets

Examination of the intraday relation for price changes of the spot and futures markets is not sufficient, equally important is intraday dynamics of the volatility of the price changes in the two markets. Chan, Chan and Karolyi (1991) pointed out that if returns volatility is time-varying, then ignoring it would amount to specification bias which ultimately would lead to incorrect inferences about lead-lag behavior of the two markets. They also argued that examining returns volatility would provide an alternative way of studying flow of information in the two markets.

This chapter presents empirical evidence regarding volatility spillovers between futures and spot markets for CNX Nifty and all of its constituents stocks. *The chapter is divided into three sections. Section 5.1 presents volatility relationship between CNX Nifty and its associated futures index. Section 5.2 presents volatility relationship between spot and futures markets for 50 individual stocks and section 5.3 gives concluding remarks.*

5.1 <u>VOLATILITY SPILLOVERS BETWEEN CNX NIFTY AND CNX NIFTY FUTURES</u>

One of the stylized facts of the financial asset returns is that the returns exhibit features of volatility clustering. There is numerous literature which supports that volatility clustering is adequately captured by Autoregressive Conditional Heteroscedasticity (ARCH) and Generalised Autoregressive Conditional Heteroscedasticity (GARCH) type models proposed by Engle (1982) and Bollerslev (1986) respectively. For studying volatility spillover mechanism, two step procedure as suggested by Tse (1999) has been used. As a first step, VECM has been estimated and residuals obtained and in the second step GARCH and VAR type models are employed. This 2-step procedure is asymptotically equal to joint estimation (Tse, 1999 p. 441). First of all, ARCH-LM test is performed to find out if there are any ARCH effects. The results of ARCH-LM test for CNX Nifty and its associated futures index are reported in Table 5.1

Table 5.1: ARCH-LM test (Full Sample)-

lags	Cash Market		Futures Market	
	χ^2-stat	p-value	χ^2-stat	p-value
1	2.6967	0.1006	0.8370	0.3603
5	8.2008	0.1455	4.7403	0.4484
10	16.1255	0.0961	11.3889	0.3280
15	16.4367	0.3536	11.8730	0.6886

Table 5.1 reveals somewhat strange results. Generally, it is expected that financial time series have ARCH effect but in the present case both the spot and futures markets do not have ARCH effect for any lag length. One possible reason for absence of ARCH effect may be inclusion of overnight returns in the sample. Figure 5.1 plots

5-min average absolute returns for CNX Nifty and its associated futures index. It is evident from the figure that the average absolute return for the first time period is substantially larger than returns in the other time intervals. This first average absolute return is the average of the absolute overnight returns. Because of these substantially larger returns, there is a large spike at a regular interval which seems to dampen ARCH effect. In other words, ARCH test captures volatility clustering and because of inclusion of overnight returns there are repeated large spikes at regular intervals which may dilute volatility clustering. To further investigate this, it is necessary to test for ARCH effect excluding overnight returns. Table 5.2 presents the results of ARCH-LM test applied on the residuals of cash and futures markets excluding overnight returns.

From Table 5.2, it is clear that both spot and futures markets have ARCH effect for various lag lengths i.e., both series have conditional heteroscedasticity. The next step is to examine volatility interactions between the two series. For studying volatility spillover, bivariate GARCH type models with constant conditional correlation have been employed.

Table 5.2: ARCH-LM Test for Sample 2-

lags	Cash Market		Futures Market	
	χ^2-stat	p-value	χ^2-stat	p-value
1	236.1913	0.0000	182.8412	0.0000
5	525.6781	0.0000	483.2949	0.0000
10	616.9619	0.0000	625.1482	0.0000
15	645.7899	0.0000	651.2609	0.0000

[Note: Sample 2 is data obtained after removing overnight returns]

Figure 5.1: 5-min average absolute returns for CNX Nifty cash and CNX Nifty Futures-

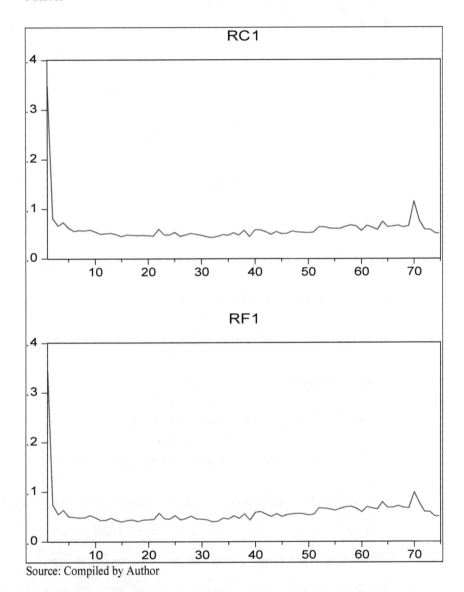

Source: Compiled by Author

Bivariate GARCH (1,1)-

The following bivariate GARCH (1,1) has been estimated:

$$\varepsilon_t = \begin{bmatrix} \varepsilon_{s,t} \\ \varepsilon_{f,t} \end{bmatrix} | \Omega_{t-1} \sim Student - t(0, H_t, v) \dots\dots (5.1)$$

$$H_t = \begin{bmatrix} \sigma_{s,t}^2 & \rho\sigma_{s,t}\sigma_{f,t} \\ \rho\sigma_{f,t}\sigma_{s,t} & \sigma_{f,t}^2 \end{bmatrix} \dots\dots\dots\dots (5.2)$$

$$\begin{bmatrix} \sigma_{s,t}^2 \\ \sigma_{f,t}^2 \end{bmatrix} = \begin{bmatrix} \omega_s \\ \omega_f \end{bmatrix} + \begin{bmatrix} \alpha_s & \gamma_f \\ \gamma_s & \alpha_f \end{bmatrix} \begin{bmatrix} \varepsilon_{s,t-1}^2 \\ \varepsilon_{f,t-1}^2 \end{bmatrix} + \begin{bmatrix} \beta_s & 0 \\ 0 & \beta_f \end{bmatrix} \begin{bmatrix} \sigma_{s,t-1}^2 \\ \sigma_{f,t-1}^2 \end{bmatrix} \dots\dots (5.3)$$

$$\sigma_{s,t}^2 = \omega_s + \alpha_s \varepsilon_{s,t-1}^2 + \gamma_f \varepsilon_{f,t-1}^2 + \beta_s \sigma_{s,t-1}^2 \dots\dots\dots (5.4)$$

$$\sigma_{f,t}^2 = \omega_f + \gamma_s \varepsilon_{s,t-1}^2 + \alpha_f \varepsilon_{f,t-1}^2 + \beta_f \sigma_{f,t-1}^2 \dots\dots\dots (5.5)$$

Where,

$\varepsilon_{s,t}, \varepsilon_{f,t}$ = residuals from VECM for the spot and futures markets respectively

Ω_{t-1} = set of information available at time t−1

H_t = variance-covariance matrix

v = degrees of freedom

ρ = coefficient of correlation between spot and futures markets

$\sigma_{s,t}^2, \sigma_{f,t}^2$ = conditional variance for the spot and futures markets respectively

In the conditional variance equation above α_s and α_f describe market specific volatility clustering for the spot and futures markets respectively. γ_f and γ_s measure volatility spillover from futures to spot market, and spot to futures market respectively. For modeling covariances, ρ denotes constant conditional correlation as in Bollerslev (1990), Chan, Chan and Karolyi (1991), Tse (1999) among others. Student-t distribution has been used for capturing excessive kurtosis and fat tails commonly exhibited by returns of financial assets.

Table 5.3 presents the results of fitting a bivariate GARCH (1,1) to the residuals of the spot and futures markets. In the table, the coefficients of prime interest are γ_s and γ_f which represents volatility spillover from spot to futures and futures to spot markets respectively.

Table 5.3: Estimates of Bivariate GARCH (1,1) for Sample 2-

	Coeff	Std.Error	t-stat	p-value
ω_s	0.0004**	0.0000	14.3472	0.0000
ω_f	0.0004**	0.0000	15.2620	0.0000
α_s	0.0802**	0.0104	7.7075	0.0000
γ_f	-0.0004	0.0089	-0.0481	0.9616
γ_s	0.0484**	0.0130	3.7389	0.0002
α_f	0.0413**	0.0113	3.6661	0.0002
β_s	0.8541**	0.0070	122.6234	0.0000
β_f	0.8373**	0.0075	112.2993	0.0000
ρ	0.9351**	0.0010	944.1183	0.0000
v	5.9824**	0.1575	37.9900	0.0000

[Notes: ** denotes significance at 5% level]
[Sample 2 is data obtained after removing overnight returns]

From the table, it can be seen that γ_f = -0.0004 (p-value = 0.9616) which indicate that innovations from the futures market do not affect volatility in the spot market. γ_s = 0.0484 (p-value = 0.0002) is statistically significant at all conventional levels of significance. γ_s measures impact of innovations of spot market on the volatility of futures market. Thus, the results of bivariate GARCH (1,1) suggest that volatility spillovers run from spot to futures and not vice versa. As expected, α_i and β_i (i=s,f), which measure market-specific volatility clustering, are positive and significant for both the spot and futures markets.

To test the adequacy of the fitted model, Ljung-Box Q test (LB-Q) is performed on standardized residuals and their squares. The test results suggest that there are no serial correlation in standardized residuals and squares of standardized residuals for both the markets. Therefore, the model seems a good fit.

Table 5.4: Ljung-Box Q-stat for Standardised Residuals and Squares of Standardised Residuals for Bivariate-GARCH (Sample 2)-

Lag	$\xi_{s,t}$ LBQ	signif	$\xi_{f,t}$ LBQ	signif	$\xi_{s,t}^2$ LBQ	signif	$\xi_{f,t}^2$ LBQ	signif
1	0.0059	0.9388	0.1899	0.6630	0.5162	0.4725	1.0855	0.2975
5	1.8375	0.8711	5.8190	0.3242	10.2893	0.0674	8.9528	0.1110
10	12.7705	0.2368	13.4683	0.1987	16.2931	0.0915	13.3544	0.2045
15	14.8599	0.4616	16.5093	0.3490	18.5240	0.2361	15.5203	0.4146
20	25.7611	0.1738	26.2006	0.1593	20.2623	0.4416	25.1960	0.1940

[Notes: $\xi_{s,t}$ and $\xi_{f,t}$ are standardised residuals for the spot and futures markets respectively. Sample 2 is data obtained after removing overnight returns.]

Bivariate EGARCH (1,1) with Asymmetry-

For studying volatility spillovers along with asymmetric effects, the following formulation has been used:

$$\ln\left(\sigma_{s,t}^2\right) = \omega_s + \alpha_s G_{s,t-1} + \gamma_f G_{f,t-1} + \beta_s \ln\left(\sigma_{s,t-1}^2\right) \dots \dots \dots \dots \ (5.6)$$

$$\ln\left(\sigma_{f,t}^2\right) = \omega_f + \gamma_s G_{s,t-1} + \alpha_f G_{f,t-1} + \beta_f \ln\left(\sigma_{f,t-1}^2\right) \dots \dots \dots \ (5.7)$$

$$G_{s,t-1} = \left(\left|\xi_{s,t-1}\right| - E\left|\xi_{s,t-1}\right|\right) + \theta_s \xi_{s,t-1} \quad [\text{where } \xi_{s,t-1} = \frac{\varepsilon_{s,t-1}}{\sigma_{s,t-1}} \dots \dots \dots \dots \ (5.8)$$

$$G_{f,t-1} = \left(\left|\xi_{f,t-1}\right| - E\left|\xi_{f,t-1}\right|\right) + \theta_f \xi_{f,t-1} \quad [\text{where } \xi_{f,t-1} = \frac{\varepsilon_{f,t-1}}{\sigma_{f,t-1}} \dots \dots \ (5.9)$$

Where,

$\xi_{s,t-1}$ and $\xi_{f,t-1}$ are standardized residuals for spot and futures markets respectively

θ_s and θ_f are asymmetric coefficients for the spot and futures markets respectively

Other symbols are defined in bivariate GARCH formulation above.

Table 5.5: Bivariate EGARCH (1,1) for Sample 2-

	Coeff	Std.Error	t-stat	p-value
ω_s	-0.3522**	0.0197	-17.8521	0.0000
ω_f	-0.3939**	0.0234	-16.8362	0.0000
α_s	0.0349**	0.0141	2.4854	0.0129
γ_s	0.1385**	0.0126	10.9668	0.0000
γ_f	-0.0439**	0.0150	-2.9280	0.0034
α_f	0.2325**	0.0143	16.3028	0.0000
β_s	0.9309**	0.0038	244.7625	0.0000
β_f	0.9219**	0.0045	203.8434	0.0000
θ_1	-0.285**	0.0384	-7.4172	0.0000
θ_2	-0.1008**	0.0242	-4.1596	0.0000
ρ	0.9391**	0.0008	1118.3901	0.0000

[Notes: ** denotes significance at the 5% level.]
[Sample 2 is obtained after removing overnight returns]

Table 5.5 reports the results of maximum likelihood estimates of bivariate EGARCH (1,1) fitted to the residuals of the spot and futures markets. All the coefficients in the model are highly significant. In this model, the coefficients of interest are γ_s and γ_f which measures volatility spillover from futures to spot and spot to futures respectively. Positive γ_s and negative θ_f indicate that there is asymmetric volatility spillover from futures to spot market, i.e., if futures market declines then it causes more volatility in the spot market as compared to futures advances. γ_f is negative and statistically significant which is usually not expected. θ_s is also negative and significant. Negative θ_s indicates that there is asymmetric volatility spillover from spot to futures market. To test the adequacy of the fitted model, diagnostics are performed using Ljung-Box Q test on the standardized residuals and squares of standardized residuals and are results are reported in Table 5.6. Standardized residuals are found to be serially uncorrelated but their squares are not. Therefore, in this case, bivariate-EGARCH (1,1) does not capture the entire volatility dynamics.

Table 5.6: Ljung-Box Q-stat for Standardised Residuals and Squares of Standardised Residuals for Bivariate-EGARCH (Sample 2)-

Lag	$\xi_{s,t}$		$\xi_{f,t}$		$\xi_{s,t}^2$		$\xi_{f,t}^2$	
	LBQ	signif	LBQ	signif	LBQ	signif	LBQ	signif
1	0.0188	0.8909	0.1557	0.6931	3.5701	0.0588	3.3271	0.0681
5	1.8188	0.8736	5.9988	0.3063	16.2600	0.0061	15.2131	0.0095
10	11.8397	0.2959	13.3692	0.2038	24.2839	0.0069	23.2687	0.0098
15	13.4197	0.5699	15.8108	0.3947	27.0878	0.0280	25.9720	0.0383
20	25.0973	0.1977	26.9144	0.1377	29.3459	0.0812	41.3098	0.0034

[Notes: Sample 2 is obtained after removing overnight returns]

Volatility Spillover after removing first and last 30 minutes-

In the opening and closing hours of a trading day, financial markets generally behave differently. For this reason, volatility linkages have also been studied after removing first and last 30-minutes of data. First of all, ARCH-LM test is conducted to find out if there are any ARCH effects in the two time series. Table 5.7 presents the results of ARCH-LM test. It is clear that both spot and futures series have ARCH effects.

Table 5.7: ARCH-LM Test for Sample 3-

lags	Cash Market		Futures Market	
	χ^2-stat	p-value	χ^2-stat	p-value
1	199.6028,	0.0000	205.6979,	0.0000
5	547.1964,	0.0000	522.5711,	0.0000
10	668.8163,	0.0000	650.6328,	0.0000
15	698.327,	0.0000	674.0557,	0.0000

[Notes: Sample 3 is obtained after removing the data for the first and last 30-minutes]

Next, to examine the volatility linkages between the two markets bivariate-GARCH and bivariate-EGARCH models have been employed. The estimates of the two models are presented in Table 5.8 and Table 5.10 respectively. In the two tables, the coefficients of prime interest are γ_s and γ_f. Table 5.8 which displays the estimates of bivariate-GARCH indicates that both γ_s and γ_f are statistically significant. This implies that volatility spillovers run in both the directions. Similarly, Table 5.10

reveals that volatility spillovers takes place in both the directions, i.e., from spot to futures and vice versa. Besides, the results of bivariate-EGARCH suggest that there is asymmetric response of volatility. Table 5.9 and 5.11 shows diagnostics performed for bivariate-GARCH and bivariate-EGARCH models respectively. The Ljung-Box Q test reveals that standardized residuals are serially uncorrelated but their squares are not serially uncorrelated. For a proper fit, both standardized residuals and their squares should be serially uncorrelated. Most previous studies including Chan, Chan, and Karolyi (1991), and Tse (1999) also report unsatisfactory diagnostics results. These studies have used a simple alternative of comparing the excess kurtosis of the raw returns and standardized residuals to assess whether the model is a good fit. Both these studies have found substantial reduction in excess kurtosis of standardized residuals and concluded that the model is a reasonable fit. In the present study also, the excess kurtosis of the standardized residuals for both the spot and futures markets is substantially smaller than that of the raw returns. These results indicate that bivariate-GARCH and bivariate-EGARCH models capture a substantial but not all portion of volatility dynamics.

Table 5.8: Bivariate GARCH (1,1) for Sample 3-

Variable	Coeff	StdError	T-Stat	Signif
ω_s	0.0004**	0.0000	11.4990	0.0000
ω_f	0.0004**	0.0000	11.6609	0.0000
α_s	0.047**	0.0111	4.2338	0.0000
γ_f	0.0238**	0.0099	2.3933	0.0167
γ_s	0.0266**	0.0133	2.0046	0.0450
α_f	0.0571**	0.0119	4.7931	0.0000
β_s	0.8525**	0.0098	86.6200	0.0000
β_f	0.8318**	0.0110	75.4748	0.0000
ρ	0.9406**	0.0010	950.1600	0.0000
ν	6.5638**	0.2072	31.6722	0.0000

[Notes: ** denotes significance at 5% level]
[Sample 3 is obtained after removing the data for the first and last 30-minutes]

Table 5.9: Ljung-Box Q-stat for Standardised Residuals and Squares of Standardised Residuals for Bivariate-GARCH (Sample 3)-

Lag	LBQ	signif	LBQ	signif	LBQ	signif	LBQ	signif
1	0.1071	0.7434	0.1431	0.7052	1.4026	0.2363	3.0641	0.0800
5	2.9497	0.7077	4.1404	0.5294	21.4852	0.0007	13.6823	0.0178
10	14.7980	0.1396	13.5478	0.2590	22.8883	0.0112	16.2940	0.0915
15	20.7452	0.1452	20.7174	0.1461	24.6656	0.0546	18.7461	0.2255
20	28.8798	0.0902	27.2667	0.1279	37.5143	0.0101	41.5081	0.0032

Notes: Sample 3 is obtained after removing the data for the first and last 30-minutes

Table 5.10: Bivariate EGARCH (1,1) for Sample 3-

Variable	Coeff	StdError	T-Stat	Signif
ω_s	-0.4094**	0.0255	-16.0363	0.0000
ω_f	-0.4565**	0.0343	-13.3169	0.0000
α_s	0.0253**	0.0081	3.1286	0.0018
γ_s	0.1336**	0.0098	13.6671	0.0000
γ_f	-0.0466**	0.0010	-45.2324	0.0000
α_f	0.2312**	0.0066	35.0900	0.0000
β_s	0.9213**	0.0047	197.9930	0.0000
β_f	0.9106**	0.0064	141.3085	0.0000
θ_1	-0.3164**	0.0454	-6.9737	0.0000
θ_2	-0.0904**	0.0183	-4.9369	0.0000
ρ	0.9459**	0.0008	1229.5076	0.0000

Notes: ** denotes significance at the 5% level.
Sample 3 is obtained after removing the data for the first and last 30-minutes

Table 5.11: Ljung-Box Q-stat for Standardised Residuals and Squares of Standardised Residuals for Bivariate-EGARCH (Sample 3)-

Lag	LBQ	p-value	LBQ	p-value	LBQ	p-value	LBQ	p-value
1	0.0698	0.7916	0.0793	0.7782	5.2724	0.0217	6.3848	0.0115
5	3.0013	0.6998	4.3276	0.5033	38.7866	0.0000	24.0151	0.0002
10	15.0459	0.1304	14.5145	0.1508	45.2861	0.0000	32.9496	0.0003
15	20.6551	0.1482	21.4853	0.1220	48.6211	0.0000	35.6242	0.0020
20	28.4200	0.0998	27.8286	0.1135	67.3701	0.0000	70.4312	0.0000

[Notes: Sample 3 is obtained after removing the data for the first and last 30-minutes]

Volatility Spillovers based on Vector Autoregressive (VAR) Model-

To complement the results from bivariate GARCH family of models, bivariate VAR model has also been used for studying volatility spillover between CNX Nifty and its associated futures contract. The following VAR has been estimated:

$$\varepsilon_{s,t}^2 = \phi_s + \sum_{i=1}^{k} \alpha_i \varepsilon_{s,t-i}^2 + \sum_{i=1}^{k} \beta_i \varepsilon_{f,t-1}^2 + \eta_{s,t} \dots \dots \dots (5.10)$$

$$\varepsilon_{f,t}^2 = \phi_f + \sum_{i=1}^{k} \gamma_i \varepsilon_{s,t-1}^2 + \sum_{i=1}^{k} \delta_i \varepsilon_{f,t-1}^2 + \eta_{f,t} \dots \dots \dots (5.11)$$

Where,

$\varepsilon_{s,t}^2, \varepsilon_{f,t}^2$ = residuals from VECM for spot and futures markets respectively

$\eta_{s,t}, \eta_{f,t}$ = white noise error terms

In the above formulation if all β_i are jointly found to be zero, then it would imply that there is no volatility spillover from futures to spot market. Similarly, if all γ_i are all jointly zero, it would mean that there is no volatility spillover from spot to futures market. Table 5.12 reports the results of pairwise Granger Causality Test for three different samples.

From the table, it can be seen that for full sample, both p-values are well above 0.05 and 0.10 indicating that the null hypothesis of no volatility spillover cannot be rejected. Thus, on the basis of Granger causality test, it can be concluded that for full sample no volatility spillovers take place between spot and futures markets. For sample 2 (removing overnight returns) the null hypothesis that spot market volatility does not spillover to futures market can be rejected only at 10% level of significance.

Similarly, the null hypothesis that no volatility spillovers take place from futures to spot market can easily be rejected at all conventional levels of significance as p-value is very small. Thus, for sample 2, it can be concluded that volatility spillovers run from futures to spot market. For sample 3 (excluding first and last 30-min), it is found that volatility spillovers run in both the directions.

Table 5.12: Granger Causality for Volatility Spillovers-

	Sample 1		Sample 2		Sample 3	
	F-test	p-value	F-test	p-value	F-test	p-value
No volatility spillover from spot to futures	1.4047	0.2359	1.7619	0.0902	2.6643	0.0094
No volatility spillover from futures to spot	0.0439	0.8341	6.6796	0.0000	1.9668	0.0555

[Notes: Sample 1 denotes the full sample; Sample 2 denotes sample obtained after removing overnight returns; and Sample 3 denotes sample obtained after removing first and last 30-minutes]

5.2 VOLATILITY SPILLOVERS FOR INDIVIDUAL STOCKS

The issue of volatility spillover has also been examined at the level of individual stocks. For examining volatility spillover bivariate vector autoregressive (VAR) model has been used. For individual stocks, the multivariate GARCH family of models has not been used. The reason is that for many stocks, the GARCH family of models did not converge. Hence, the analysis has been restricted to VAR only. The following VAR has been estimated and Granger causality test conducted on the estimated VAR.

$$\varepsilon_{s,t}^2 = \phi_s + \sum_{i=1}^{k} \alpha_i \varepsilon_{s,t-i}^2 + \sum_{i=1}^{k} \beta_i \varepsilon_{f,t-1}^2 + \eta_{s,t} \ldots \ldots \ldots (5.12)$$

$$\varepsilon_{f,t}^2 = \phi_f + \sum_{i=1}^{k} \gamma_i \varepsilon_{s,t-1}^2 + \sum_{i=1}^{k} \delta_i \varepsilon_{f,t-1}^2 + \eta_{f,t} \ldots\ldots\ldots\ldots (5.13)$$

Where,

$\varepsilon_{s,t}^2, \varepsilon_{f,t}^2$ = residuals from VECM for spot and futures markets respectively

$\eta_{s,t}, \eta_{f,t}$ = white noise error terms

In the above formulation if all β_i are jointly found to be zero, then it would imply that there is no volatility spillover from futures to spot market. Similarly, if all γ_i are all jointly zero, it would mean that there is no volatility spillover from spot to futures market. The results of Granger causality are discussed in the following sections.

Volatility Spilllovers for Full Sample-

Table 5.13 presents results of Granger causality test for full sample. From the table it can be seen that out of 50 stocks, 41 stocks (38 stocks at 5% level and 3 stocks at 10% level) have significant volatility spillovers from futures to spot market. For BPCL, HINDALCO, HINDUNILVR, INFY, ONGC, SBIN, TATAMOTORS, TATAPOWER, and TATASTEEL volatility does not spillover from futures to spot market. As far as volatility spillover from spot to futures market is concerned, 26 stocks (22 stocks at 5% level and 4 stocks at 10% level) have significant volatility spillover from spot to futures market. Besides, it is found that for 25 stocks volatility spillovers take place in both directions, i.e., from spot to futures market, and from futures to spot market.

Table 5.13: Granger Causality Test for Full Sample-

Company	Spot does not Granger Cause Futures		Futures does not Granger Cause Spot	
	F-test	p-value	F-test	p-value
ACC	26.9462**	0.0000	1.0974	0.3338
AMBUJACEM	5.7704**	0.0000	6.1324**	0.0000
AXISBANK	6.1538**	0.0131	0.9647	0.3260
BAJAJAUTO	8.8822**	0.0000	2.3859*	0.0671
BHARTIARTL	29.07**	0.0000	10.6166**	0.0000
BHEL	7.0348**	0.0000	1.0283	0.3989
BPCL	0.1021	0.7493	0.1109	0.7392
CAIRN	38.9353**	0.0000	977.3589**	0.0000
CIPLA	30.5237**	0.0000	21.0117**	0.0000
COALINDIA	3.0884**	0.0456	4.6563**	0.0095
DLF	3.391*	0.0656	0.8478	0.3572
DRREDDY	4.2659**	0.0389	2.0077	0.1565
GAIL	14.8174**	0.0000	61.5318**	0.0000
GRASIM	107.6625**	0.0000	17.8723**	0.0000
HCLTECH	7.2489**	0.0001	12.3902**	0.0000
HDFC	6.7566**	0.0000	42.227**	0.0000
HDFCBANK	3.8689**	0.0007	7.797**	0.0000
HEROMOTOCO	6.5949**	0.0000	8.171**	0.0000
HINDALCO	0.0163	0.8985	0.0021	0.9633
HINDUNILVR	0.424	0.6544	0.1973	0.8210
ICICIBANK	3.2105*	0.0732	0.0018	0.9663
IDFC	8.7041**	0.0032	2.7448*	0.0976
INFY	2.411	0.1205	2.2764	0.1314
ITC	4.1699**	0.0412	0.0046	0.9459
JINDALSTEL	48.8315**	0.0000	21.8673**	0.0000
JPASSOCIAT	4.0586**	0.0440	1.0568	0.3040
KOTAKBANK	4.1003**	0.0010	0.5806	0.7150
LT	4.0809**	0.0434	0.0001	0.9903
M&M	34.1879**	0.0000	2.2591	0.1045
MARUTI	22.0289**	0.0000	4.8279**	0.0280
NTPC	38.7492**	0.0000	1.8207*	0.0908
ONGC	0.1769	0.6740	0.2212	0.6381
PNB	38.0262**	0.0000	8.2719**	0.0040
POWERGRID	80.4375**	0.0000	1.6994	0.1167
RANBAXY	11.979**	0.0005	2.2116	0.1370
RCOM	4.1807**	0.0003	2.4248**	0.0241
RELIANCE	9.5306**	0.0020	6.4666**	0.0110
RELINFRA	23.4346**	0.0000	10.2582**	0.0000
RPOWER	43.9572**	0.0000	1.6599	0.1976

SAIL	20.0594**	0.0000	2.1518	0.1163
SBIN	2.1417	0.1433	1.8649	0.1721
SESAGOA	46.3841**	0.0000	21.2598**	0.0000
SIEMENS	2.5621*	0.0530	6.5146**	0.0002
STER	26.0966**	0.0000	3.3944**	0.0171
SUNPHARMA	33.5184**	0.0000	14.044**	0.0002
TATAMOTORS	0.0083	0.9274	0.1128	0.7370
TATAPOWER	0.2463	0.6197	0.3977	0.5283
TATASTEEL	1.1463	0.2843	3.2764*	0.0703
TCS	18.6305**	0.0000	2.1771	0.1401
WIPRO	25.7127**	0.0000	23.3894**	0.0000

[Notes: ** and * denote significance at 5% and 10% level respectively]

Volatility Spillovers after excluding overnight returns-

Overnight returns are larger in magnitude than intraday returns. For this reason, volatility spillovers have also been examined after removing overnight returns. The results of Granger causality test based on VAR are reported in Table 5.14. The null hypothesis that spot volatility, represented by squares of innovations from the first step VECM, does not Granger cause volatility in the futures market is rejected for 48 (45 stocks at 5% level and 3 stocks at 10% level) out of 50 stocks. TCS and AXISBANK are the only two stocks for which spot market volatility does not Granger cause futures market volatility. Again, the null hypothesis that futures market volatility does not Granger cause spot market volatility is rejected for 46 stocks (45 stocks at 5% level and 1 stock at 10% level). JPASSOCIAT, LT, RELIANCE and SESAGOA are the four stocks for which futures market volatility does not Granger cause volatility in the spot market. Out of 50 stocks, 44 stocks have bidirectional volatility spillovers.

Table 5.14: Granger Causality Test for Sample 2-

Company	Spot does not Granger Cause Futures		Futures does not Granger Cause Spot	
	F-test	p-value	F-test	p-value
ACC	5.88**	0.0028	9.2475**	0.0001
AMBUJACEM	68.5435**	0.0000	24.2392**	0.0000
AXISBANK	0.243	0.9140	2.2528*	0.0608
BAJAJAUTO	68.6171**	0.0000	6.0338**	0.0004
BHARTIARTL	8.2439**	0.0000	11.747**	0.0000
BHEL	11.0913**	0.0000	13.0104**	0.0000
BPCL	7.9427**	0.0000	17.1138**	0.0000
CAIRN	16.0006**	0.0000	18.2835**	0.0000
CIPLA	10.2001**	0.0000	3.1945**	0.0069
COALINDIA	11.3745**	0.0000	10.3564**	0.0000
DLF	25.1782**	0.0000	23.9613**	0.0000
DRREDDY	21.5241**	0.0000	11.4669**	0.0000
GAIL	24.2224**	0.0000	116.6393**	0.0000
GRASIM	9.8365**	0.0000	6.5211**	0.0000
HCLTECH	3.3801**	0.0090	3.9759**	0.0032
HDFC	4.7807**	0.0000	83.2266**	0.0000
HDFCBANK	46.2947**	0.0000	88.3019**	0.0000
HEROMOTOCO	1.6833*	0.0968	6.8385**	0.0000
HINDALCO	4.005**	0.0073	6.4476**	0.0002
HINDUNILVR	39.7462**	0.0000	37.8164**	0.0000
ICICIBANK	5.2519**	0.0000	25.5592**	0.0000
IDFC	4.3281**	0.0047	2.7277**	0.0424
INFY	7.8484**	0.0000	6.3549**	0.0000
ITC	1.9982*	0.0623	2.7569**	0.0111
JINDALSTEL	3.875**	0.0088	68.9456**	0.0000
JPASSOCIAT	5.0204**	0.0018	0.8284	0.4780
KOTAKBANK	5.9771**	0.0005	6.7745**	0.0001
LT	4.7161**	0.0003	1.573	0.1639
M&M	5.307**	0.0000	2.6167**	0.0035
MARUTI	33.8104**	0.0000	11.6952**	0.0000
NTPC	5.7934**	0.0000	2.7496**	0.0075
ONGC	7.5982**	0.0000	10.4766**	0.0000
PNB	5.8424**	0.0029	9.1337**	0.0001
POWERGRID	6.2855**	0.0003	14.7253**	0.0000
RANBAXY	10.4126**	0.0000	14.6333**	0.0000
RCOM	7.8887**	0.0000	6.4741**	0.0000
RELIANCE	3.167**	0.0073	1.6946	0.1320
RELINFRA	16.2118**	0.0000	13.1089**	0.0000
RPOWER	2.9777**	0.0040	2.6479**	0.0098

SAIL	36.3393**	0.0000	6.8201**	0.0011
SBIN	26.5241**	0.0000	23.772**	0.0000
SESAGOA	11.0232**	0.0000	0.9721	0.4047
SIEMENS	1.9916*	0.0631	10.9032**	0.0000
STER	6.0818**	0.0004	2.7859**	0.0392
SUNPHARMA	2.4265**	0.0457	14.8997**	0.0000
TATAMOTORS	4.7529**	0.0026	11.098**	0.0000
TATAPOWER	4.6806**	0.0093	9.8251**	0.0001
TATASTEEL	9.5406**	0.0000	12.3613**	0.0000
TCS	0.7197	0.5783	6.1886**	0.0001
WIPRO	9.4854**	0.0000	27.4139**	0.0000

[Notes: ** and * denote significance at 5% and 10% level respectively]

Volatility Spillover after excluding first and last 30 minutes-

It is generally observed that there is excessive volatility at the open and close of a trading session due to various reasons including asymmetric flow of information. For this reason, volatility spillovers have also been studied after removing data for the first and last 30 minutes. Table 5.15 summarizes the results of Granger causality test applied on the squares of residuals from the spot and futures markets. From the table, it is evident that for 37 stocks the null hypothesis that spot market volatility does not granger cause futures market volatility is rejected. The null hypothesis of no granger causality from futures market to spot market is rejected for 41 stocks. In addition, for 30 stocks volatility spillover takes place in both the directions.

5.3 CONCLUSION

This chapter has examined the intraday returns volatility relationship between spot and futures markets in India. More specifically, it is examined whether volatility from one market transmits to other market or not. First, for studying the volatility transmission mechanism of CNX Nifty and its associated futures contract, GARCH type models are employed.

Table 5.15: Granger Causality Test for Sample 3-

Company	Spot does not Granger Cause Futures		Futures does not Granger Cause Spot	
	F-test	p-value	F-test	p-value
ACC	0.1994	0.8968	2.8518**	0.0358
AMBUJACEM	0.4258	0.5141	9.7184**	0.0018
AXISBANK	0.9372	0.4216	13.0592**	0.0000
BAJAJAUTO	1.0419	0.3528	0.8354	0.4337
BHARTIARTL	1.1309	0.3350	1.0908	0.3515
BHEL	1.1411	0.3195	12.0448**	0.0000
BPCL	1.1867	0.3131	20.5393**	0.0000
CAIRN	1.5202	0.2070	8.5547**	0.0000
CIPLA	1.588	0.1899	11.6573**	0.0000
COALINDIA	1.8983	0.1275	5.6405**	0.0007
DLF	2.0176	0.1091	4.5313**	0.0035
DRREDDY	2.1393	0.1178	6.6939**	0.0012
GAIL	2.631	0.1048	33.2136**	0.0000
GRASIM	2.7021**	0.0439	1.8253	0.1401
HCLTECH	2.815*	0.0599	0.7719	0.4621
HDFC	2.8826**	0.0344	3.2503**	0.0208
HDFCBANK	3.4155**	0.0023	7.3664**	0.0000
HEROMOTOCO	3.6183**	0.0028	8.5361**	0.0000
HINDALCO	3.8479**	0.0017	3.1736**	0.0072
HINDUNILVR	3.8956**	0.0085	0.7673	0.5122
ICICIBANK	3.8997**	0.0016	4.5514**	0.0004
IDFC	4.0403**	0.0001	4.6169**	0.0000
INFY	4.2339**	0.0001	5.6426**	0.0000
ITC	4.6863**	0.0009	3.9916**	0.0031
JINDALSTEL	4.8301**	0.0023	4.2261**	0.0054
JPASSOCIAT	4.8472**	0.0079	15.0523**	0.0000
KOTAKBANK	5.0574**	0.0245	14.4061**	0.0001
LT	5.0709**	0.0016	31.277**	0.0000
M&M	6.041**	0.0004	1.7853	0.1475
MARUTI	6.0641**	0.0004	4.0355**	0.0070
NTPC	6.6758**	0.0013	1.0501	0.3499
ONGC	6.6877**	0.0002	15.7078**	0.0000
PNB	7.5611**	0.0000	29.7522**	0.0000
POWERGRID	8.7673**	0.0000	7.35**	0.0001
RANBAXY	9.7508**	0.0000	0.7502	0.5577
RCOM	10.3018**	0.0000	12.0395**	0.0000
RELIANCE	10.568**	0.0000	1.0317	0.4022
RELINFRA	11.6076**	0.0000	3.2516**	0.0208
RPOWER	12.0184**	0.0000	7.76**	0.0000

SAIL	12.2154**	0.0000	45.2748**	0.0000
SBIN	15.7554**	0.0000	7.3574**	0.0001
SESAGOA	21.6299**	0.0000	19.4585**	0.0000
SIEMENS	32.1408**	0.0000	10.4062**	0.0000
STER	32.6088**	0.0000	93.3125**	0.0000
SUNPHARMA	34.1621**	0.0000	20.8385**	0.0000
TATAMOTORS	35.8297**	0.0000	57.4083**	0.0000
TATAPOWER	49.0265**	0.0000	12.2357**	0.0000
TATASTEEL	52.1467**	0.0000	12.7694**	0.0000
TCS	61.327**	0.0000	37.1399**	0.0000
WIPRO	151.4276**	0.0000	3.1698**	0.0420

[Notes: ** and * denote significance at 5% and 10% level respectively]
[Sample 3 denotes data obtained after removing data for the first and last 30-minutes]

For studying the volatility dynamics three different sample specifications are considered, viz., sample 1 (full sample), sample 2 (sample after removing overnight returns), and sample 3 (sample after removing returns for the first and last 30-minutes). For the full time period, returns are found to have no ARCH effects. For sample 2, Bivariate-GARCH model indicates that volatility spillovers run from spot market to futures market but not in the reverse direction. However, the result of bivariate EGARCH (1,1) proposes that volatility spillovers take place in both the directions, i.e., volatility transmits from spot to futures and from futures to spot. It is also found that volatility transmission mechanism is asymmetric in nature, i.e., market declines cause more volatility than market advances.

To complement the results of GARCH-type models, the volatility spillover mechanism has also been examined in the framework of a vector autoregressive (VAR) model. For CNX Nifty spot and futures index, the results of Granger causality test are different for the three samples considered. For the full sample, it is found that no volatility spillovers take place between the two markets. For sample 2, it is found that volatility spillovers run from futures to spot market and not vice versa. For sample 3, the Granger Causality test suggests that volatility spillover takes place in both the directions, i.e., from spot to futures market and vice versa.

In addition, the volatility spillover mechanism at the level of individual stocks has also been examined. Again, the whole series of examination has been performed with three different sample, i.e., full sample, sample after removing overnight returns, and sample after excluding first and last 30-minutes. For majority of the stocks, it has been found that volatility spillovers take place between both the markets. However, spillovers from futures to spot market are found to be more pronounced.

Overall, it is found that price innovations originating in either of the two markets are helpful in predicting the future volatility in the other market. The results of the study indicate strong inter-market linkages in the returns volatility of the spot and futures markets.

Chapter-6
Findings and Conclusion

Relationship between spot and futures markets has been an area of vast empirical investigation in the last few decades. Although considerable attention has been paid to examine the relationship between stock index and stock index futures, only a few studies have examined the relationship between individual stock and stock futures. Besides, most of the previous studies have examined only first moment relationship, that is, lead-lag relationship between a market index and its associated futures contract.

The present study is an attempt to fill this gap to some extent. The study examines first and second moment relationships between spot and futures markets for CNX Nifty and all of its constituent stocks. More specifically, the study addresses the following questions:

- Do spot and futures markets have a long-run equilibrium relationship? In other words, are spot and futures markets cointegrated?

- Does there exist any lead-lag relationship between spot and futures price changes?

- Does volatility in one market affect volatility in another market?

To answer the abovementioned questions, the study has used 5-min transaction price data from June 1, 2012 to May 31, 2013 and employed a number of tools & techniques of time series econometrics.

This chapter is organized as follows. Section 6.1 presents a summary of the findings along with conclusion. Section 6.2 states the major limitations of the study and finally, section 6.3 suggests areas for further research.

6.1 FINDINGS AND CONCLUSION

The major findings of the study are presented below:

The results of Augmented Dickey-Fuller (ADF) test suggest that the price series of spot and futures markets for CNX Nifty and all of its fifty constituent stocks have a unit root. In other words, both the spot and futures price series in their levels are non-stationary. Besides, the ADF test suggests that first differences of log prices (returns) are stationary for all the time series considered. This implies that both spot and futures price series are integrated of the order 1, i.e., I(1).

For studying long run relationship between spot and futures markets Johansen-Juselius (1990) cointegration procedure has been employed. The results of J-J cointegration analysis suggest that spot and futures price series of CNX Nifty and all of its component stocks are cointegrated. It implies that there is long run relationship between spot and futures markets. Further, this long run relationship exists at the level of index as well as at the level of individual stocks.

For cointegrated variables, the appropriate econometric technique is Vector Error Correction Model (VECM). The whole series of examination is carried out with three sample specifications, viz., sample 1 (full sample); sample 2 (sample obtained after removing overnight returns); and sample 3 (sample obtained after removing returns for the first and last 30-minutes). For estimating the VECM for the full sample, 3 lags are found most appropriate based on Schwarz Information Criterion (SIC). The result of VECM reveals that the coefficient of the error correction term ectt−1 for ΔFt is positive and statistically significant at 10% level. However, the error correction term for ΔSt is statistically insignificant. It implies that futures market responds to correct for the disequilibrium from the long-term relationship and spot market does not. Further, the positive coefficient of ectt−1 for ΔFt implies that if futures price is relatively lower than spot price at time t−1, then it is likely to adjust upward to restore the equilibrium in the next period. Moreover, for ΔSt, own lags as well as lags of ΔFt are statistically significant. However, for ΔFt, neither own lags nor lags of ΔSt are significant except for the first lag. It implies that for predicting spot market, information for the last 15 minutes (3 lags) is important, however, for the futures market, only last 5 minutes information (1 lag) is useful.

The results of VECM for sample 2 for CNX Nifty are qualitatively similar to that of the full sample. It is the futures market which has the tendency to adjust to correct the deviation from the equilibrium relationship. However, if we look at the size and significance of lagged coefficients then it is evident that spot market has a memory of 15 to 25 minutes but futures market has a memory of only 5 minutes.

For sample 3, it is found that error correction takes place in both the markets. Again, if we examine individual coefficients then for ΔSt all the lags (3 in this case) from the spot and futures markets are significant, and for ΔFt only one lag is significant. This indicates that for predicting futures market returns only past 5-min returns information from the spot market is important and any older information is not important.

Besides, the error correction mechanism is also studied after partitioning the one year intraday data into many smaller sub periods. For different sub-periods, it is found that most of the times it is the futures market which adjusts to correct the deviation from the long-run equilibrium relationship. For a few sub periods spot market is also found to react to correct the disequilibrium. Further, it is also found that for a few sub periods, both the markets adjust to restore the equilibrium relationship.

Further, to examine the direction of flow of information between spot and futures markets, Granger Causality test has been applied based on Vector Autoregression (VAR). The null hypothesis that futures market does not granger cause spot market is rejected at 5% level of significance for all the three samples. Similarly, the null hypothesis that spot market does not granger cause futures market is also rejected for all the three sample specifications. It implies that for CNX Nifty, spot and futures markets have feedback relationship and significant information transmission takes place between the two markets.

The error correction mechanism for the individual stocks that comprises the CNX Nifty reveals that for most of the stocks it is the futures market which adjusts to correct the deviation from the long run equilibrium relationship. This behavior of individual stocks corroborates the behavior of CNX Nifty.

The short term temporal relationship between the futures and spot markets for all the fifty stocks of CNX Nifty is carried out in the framework of VAR. The null hypothesis that spot market does not granger cause futures market is rejected for all the 50 stocks. Similarly, the null hypothesis that futures market does not granger cause spot market is also rejected. It implies that both spot and futures markets granger cause each other indicating that feedback relationship exists between the two markets. This indicates that past history of spot market returns is helpful in predicting returns from the futures market and vice versa. Thus, a feedback relationship exists between futures and spot markets for all the 50 constituent stocks. However, an examination of the size and significance of the lagged coefficients in the VAR model points that causality from futures to spot market is much stronger than in the reverse direction. Lead-lag relationship between spot and futures return series of individual stocks has also been examined after removing first and last 30-min data. BHARTIARTL is the only stock for which there is no granger causality from futures to spot market, otherwise for all other stocks there runs granger causality from spot to futures and futures to spot markets.

The results of ARCH-LM test suggest that for sample 1, CNX Nifty and its futures contract both do not have ARCH effects. Mostly, financial time series suffer from conditional heteroscedasticity. However, in this case, the absence of ARCH effects may be due to inclusion of overnight returns in sample 1. For sample 2 and sample 3 it is found that both CNX Nifty and its futures contract have ARCH effects. The results for sample 2 & 3 are consistent with commonly observed volatility clustering in financial assets' returns.

For sample 2, Bivariate-GARCH (1,1) model with constant conditional correlation suggests that volatility spillovers run from spot to futures market and not vice versa. However, The results of Bivariate-EGARCH (1,1) reveal that volatility spillovers take place in both the directions.

For sample 3, Bivariate-GARCH and Bivariate-EGARCH both models suggest that volatility spillovers run in both the directions. Therefore, innovations in either of the markets are helpful in predicting volatility in another market.

For both sample 1 and 2, the results of bivariate-EGARCH suggest that there is asymmetric response of volatility.

Volatility linkages are also examined using Granger Causality test based on VAR. For CNX Nifty, the results of Granger Causality are mixed. On the basis of the Granger causality test, it is found that for full sample no volatility spillovers take place between spot and futures markets. For sample 2 (removing overnight returns) the null hypothesis that spot market volatility does not spillover to futures market is rejected only at 10% level of significance. However, the null hypothesis that no volatility spillovers take place from futures to spot market is rejected at all conventional levels of significance. Thus, for sample 2, it can be concluded that volatility spillovers run from futures to spot market. For sample 3 (excluding first and last 30-min), it is found that volatility spillovers run in both the directions.

The issue of volatility spillover has also been examined at the level of individual stocks. For examining volatility spillover bivariate vector autoregressive (VAR) model has been used. For sample 1, it is found that for 41 stocks volatility spillovers run from futures to spot market and for 26 stocks volatility spillovers run in the reverse direction. For 25 stocks, volatility is found to run in both the directions.

For sample 2, the results of Granger Causality suggest that for 48 out of 50 stocks volatility spillovers run from spot to futures market and for 46 stocks volatility spillovers run from futures to spot market. Besides, 44 stocks have bidirectional volatility spillovers.

For sample 3, it is found that for 37 stocks volatility spillovers take place from spot to futures market. The null hypothesis of no granger causality from futures market to spot market is rejected for 41 stocks. In addition, for 30 stocks volatility spillover takes place in both the directions.

The present study is an attempt to characterize the intraday returns and volatility relationships between futures and spot markets in India. It is found that there exists strong long-run relationship between the spot and futures markets at the level of index as well as at the level of individual stocks. Price discovery takes place in both the markets. Further, futures market is found to play a dominant role in the matter of price discovery. These findings are consistent with previous researches in India as well as abroad.

As far as the volatility linkages between futures and spot markets are concerned, the present study has come up with mixed results. Previously in the Indian markets, Karmakar (2009) employed BEKK-GARCH to show that for CNX Nifty volatility of futures market spills over to the spot market and not vice versa. However, he utilized daily data and for uncovering volatility dynamics intraday data are more appropriate. In a similar study, Pati and Rajib (2011) employed 5-min intraday data and found that for CNX Nifty volatility spillovers run in both directions. However, they also reported stronger role of futures market as compared to spot market.

Present study highlights an important characteristic of time series models. For studying volatility dynamics, the study has utilized three different models, viz., Bivariate-GARCH, Bivariate-EGARCH with asymmetry and VAR. In addition, the mechanism of volatility linkages is studied with three sample specifications viz., sample 1 (full sample); sample 2 (sample obtained after removing overnight returns); and sample 3 (sample obtained after removing returns for the first and last 30-minutes). Interestingly, different models yielded different results and even the same model obtained different results for different sample specifications. This implies that generalizing on the basis of a-theoretic time series models should be done with great caution. Moreover, this also underlines the inherent complexity in modeling higher order linkages such as second order linkages i.e., volatility spillovers. Besides, variability in results due to change of model and/or change of sample also points towards unpredictability of financial markets and market efficiency.

In conclusion, it can be said that both futures and spot markets serve price discovery function. Spot and futures markets are found to be linked through their first and second moments. It indicates that significant returns and volatility relationship exist between the two markets. These findings may prove to be useful by providing insight on price discovery and have implications for understanding information transmission mechanism and thereby assisting hedgers, arbitrageurs and portfolio managers in executing trading strategies.

6.2 LIMITATIONS OF THE STUDY

Besides the usual limitations of time and resources, the major limitations of the study are as follows:

- High frequency data is not easily available. The present study has used intraday data for only one year. Data for a longer time period would yield better results.
- For studying returns and volatility relationship corporate actions such as payments of dividends etc. have not been considered.
- Autoregressive family of models are generally a-theoretical in nature. Generalizing on the basis of these models should be done with great caution.

6.3 AREAS FOR FUTURE RESEARCH

The areas for future research are as follows:

- First, the study with a longer time span can be conducted.

- The future studies may use data at even higher frequency such as 1-minute.

- Returns and volatility relationship between spot and options markets and between futures and options markets are yet another prominent areas of research.

- Returns andVolatility spillovers among different stock markets of two or more countries can also be studied.

- Impact of trading activity on volatility spillovers among markets is another good area for future research.

- With the advancements in econometric techniques, future researches may be conducted utilizing newer techniques.

APPENDIX- I

Table 4A.1: Results of ADF Test for Individual Stocks-

ACC	-2.009	0.283	-2.010	0.283	-139.934	0.000	-140.922	0.000
AMBUJACEM	-2.859	0.050	-3.060	0.030	-93.041	0.000	-137.249	0.000
AXISBANK	-1.318	0.623	-1.436	0.566	-140.051	0.000	-140.299	0.000
BAJAJ-AUTO	-1.804	0.379	-1.781	0.390	-143.102	0.000	-142.767	0.000
BHARTIARTL	-1.672	0.446	-1.656	0.454	-142.789	0.000	-144.599	0.000
BHEL	-1.493	0.537	-1.495	0.536	-138.008	0.000	-138.315	0.000
BPCL	-2.410	0.139	-2.423	0.135	-136.624	0.000	-138.354	0.000
CAIRN	-1.676	0.444	-1.603	0.481	-139.492	0.000	-142.504	0.000
CIPLA	-2.183	0.213	-2.150	0.225	-137.874	0.000	-139.618	0.000
COALINDIA	-1.752	0.405	-1.662	0.451	-98.830	0.000	-142.614	0.000
DLF	-1.851	0.356	-1.890	0.337	-137.708	0.000	-137.578	0.000
DRREDDY	-0.745	0.833	-0.746	0.833	-142.702	0.000	-142.959	0.000
GAIL	-1.957	0.306	-1.929	0.319	-98.285	0.000	-99.294	0.000
GRASIM	-2.740	0.067	-2.675	0.078	-138.848	0.000	-139.343	0.000
HCLTECH	-0.965	0.768	-0.927	0.780	-140.558	0.000	-142.946	0.000
HDFC	-1.282	0.640	-1.425	0.571	-139.261	0.000	-140.324	0.000
HDFCBANK	-2.576	0.098	-2.689	0.076	-143.232	0.000	-145.380	0.000
HEROMOTOCO	-1.365	0.601	-1.406	0.581	-139.000	0.000	-138.134	0.000
HINDALCO	-1.707	0.427	-1.735	0.414	-126.982	0.000	-127.863	0.000
HINDUNILVR	-1.659	0.452	-1.624	0.470	-93.134	0.000	-134.933	0.000
ICICIBANK	-2.384	0.146	-2.369	0.151	-140.104	0.000	-140.585	0.000
IDFC	-2.207	0.204	-2.179	0.214	-137.404	0.000	-138.989	0.000
INFY	-1.754	0.404	-1.740	0.411	-139.398	0.000	-140.556	0.000
ITC	-1.442	0.563	-1.633	0.466	-141.103	0.000	-142.450	0.000
JINDALSTEL	-0.465	0.896	-0.404	0.906	-137.324	0.000	-140.459	0.000
JPASSOCIAT	-1.685	0.439	-1.713	0.425	-93.251	0.000	-93.635	0.000
KOTAKBANK	-0.544	0.880	-0.508	0.887	-101.666	0.000	-101.979	0.000
LT	-2.920	0.043	-2.887	0.047	-137.834	0.000	-139.947	0.000
M&M	-1.871	0.346	-1.927	0.320	-141.820	0.000	-142.704	0.000
MARUTI	-1.309	0.628	-1.266	0.648	-136.114	0.000	-137.880	0.000
NTPC	-2.127	0.234	-2.075	0.255	-137.983	0.000	-141.530	0.000
ONGC	-1.681	0.441	-1.620	0.472	-137.714	0.000	-94.672	0.000
PNB	-1.928	0.320	-1.982	0.295	-136.572	0.000	-136.213	0.000
POWERGRID	-2.665	0.080	-2.596	0.094	-138.091	0.000	-141.061	0.000
RANBAXY	-0.270	0.927	-0.340	0.917	-138.848	0.000	-138.952	0.000
RCOM	-0.226	0.933	-0.283	0.925	-92.742	0.000	-93.304	0.000
RELIANCE	-2.329	0.163	-2.311	0.169	-140.401	0.000	-141.977	0.000
RELINFRA	-0.608	0.867	-0.712	0.842	-138.115	0.000	-93.905	0.000
RPOWER	-0.734	0.836	-0.819	0.813	-139.710	0.000	-139.850	0.000
SAIL	0.194	0.972	0.112	0.967	-139.649	0.000	-142.067	0.000

SBIN	-1.654	0.455	-1.731	0.416	-139.749	0.000	-139.774	0.000
SESAGOA	-1.788	0.387	-1.778	0.392	-141.627	0.000	-140.044	0.000
SIEMENS	-1.239	0.660	-1.257	0.652	-131.102	0.000	-131.873	0.000
STER	-1.965	0.303	-2.011	0.282	-140.363	0.000	-141.022	0.000
SUNPHARMA	0.001	0.958	0.134	0.968	-140.045	0.000	-141.826	0.000
TATAMOTORS	-1.524	0.521	-1.476	0.546	-140.462	0.000	-141.527	0.000
TATAPOWER	-2.171	0.217	-2.276	0.180	-142.083	0.000	-144.106	0.000
TATASTEEL	-0.138	0.944	-0.192	0.937	-140.196	0.000	-139.241	0.000
TCS	-1.172	0.689	-1.279	0.642	-142.670	0.000	-144.483	0.000
WIPRO	-1.432	0.568	-1.376	0.596	-134.924	0.000	-137.779	0.000

Table 4A.2: J-J Cointegration test results for Individual Stocks-

Symbol	No of CE	Eigenvalue	Trace	p-value	Max-Eigen	p-value
ACC	None	0.0027	53.2731	0.0000	49.1472	0.0000
	At most 1	0.0002	4.1259	0.0422	4.1259	0.0422
AMBUJACEM	None	0.0037	77.0297	0.0000	67.6817	0.0000
	At most 1	0.0005	9.3481	0.0022	9.3481	0.0022
AXISBANK	None	0.0016	30.7127	0.0001	29.2790	0.0001
	At most 1	0.0001	1.4337	0.2312	1.4337	0.2312
BAJAJAUTO	None	0.0034	65.1109	0.0000	61.7311	0.0000
	At most 1	0.0002	3.3798	0.0660	3.3798	0.0660
BHARTIARTL	None	0.0047	88.2381	0.0000	85.4620	0.0000
	At most 1	0.0002	2.7762	0.0957	2.7762	0.0957
BHEL	None	0.0045	84.0386	0.0000	81.5022	0.0000
	At most 1	0.0001	2.5364	0.1112	2.5364	0.1112
BPCL	None	0.0046	88.6433	0.0000	82.2493	0.0000
	At most 1	0.0004	6.3940	0.0114	6.3940	0.0114
CAIRN	None	0.0023	44.7767	0.0000	42.2553	0.0000
	At most 1	0.0001	2.5215	0.1123	2.5215	0.1123
CIPLA	None	0.0045	86.0125	0.0000	81.3675	0.0000
	At most 1	0.0003	4.6450	0.0311	4.6450	0.0311
COALINDIA	None	0.0012	23.8348	0.0022	21.1975	0.0034
	At most 1	0.0001	2.6373	0.1044	2.6373	0.1044
DLF	None	0.0030	58.7355	0.0000	55.2864	0.0000
	At most 1	0.0002	3.4491	0.0633	3.4491	0.0633
DRREDDY	None	0.0031	56.0146	0.0000	55.5204	0.0000
	At most 1	0.0000	0.4942	0.4821	0.4942	0.4821
GAIL	None	0.0025	46.7232	0.0000	42.9245	0.0000
	At most 1	0.0002	3.7987	0.0513	3.7987	0.0513
GRASIM	None	0.0035	67.5682	0.0000	60.0373	0.0000
	At most 1	0.0004	7.5309	0.0061	7.5309	0.0061
HCLTECH	None	0.0042	76.0835	0.0000	75.0838	0.0000
	At most 1	0.0001	0.9996	0.3174	0.9996	0.3174
HDFC	None	0.0020	38.8770	0.0000	36.4805	0.0000
	At most 1	0.0001	2.3964	0.1216	2.3964	0.1216
HDFCBANK	None	0.0035	69.9320	0.0000	63.1164	0.0000
	At most 1	0.0004	6.8156	0.0090	6.8156	0.0090
HEROMOTOCO	None	0.0017	31.9388	0.0001	30.1556	0.0001
	At most 1	0.0001	1.7831	0.1818	1.7831	0.1818
HINDALCO	None	0.0043	68.1330	0.0000	65.2122	0.0000
	At most 1	0.0002	2.9208	0.0874	2.9208	0.0874
HINDUNILVR	None	0.0033	62.4849	0.0000	60.8759	0.0000
	At most 1	0.0001	1.6089	0.2046	1.6089	0.2046
ICICIBANK	None	0.0011	25.2829	0.0012	19.6314	0.0064
	At most 1	0.0003	5.6515	0.0174	5.6515	0.0174

IDFC	None	0.0014	30.7648	0.0001	25.7807	0.0005
	At most 1	0.0003	4.9841	0.0256	4.9841	0.0256
INFY	None	0.0015	30.1662	0.0002	27.0805	0.0003
	At most 1	0.0002	3.0857	0.0790	3.0857	0.0790
ITC	None	0.0024	44.8305	0.0000	43.3349	0.0000
	At most 1	0.0001	1.4955	0.2214	1.4955	0.2214
JINDALSTEL	None	0.0062	113.1744	0.0001	113.0090	0.0001
	At most 1	0.0000	0.1655	0.6842	0.1655	0.6842
JPASSOCIAT	None	0.0021	41.5051	0.0000	38.5677	0.0000
	At most 1	0.0002	2.9374	0.0865	2.9374	0.0865
KOTAKBANK	None	0.0054	99.4162	0.0001	99.0645	0.0000
	At most 1	0.0000	0.3518	0.5531	0.3518	0.5531
LT	None	0.0030	64.4986	0.0000	55.5644	0.0000
	At most 1	0.0005	8.9342	0.0028	8.9342	0.0028
M&M	None	0.0022	43.9706	0.0000	40.3715	0.0000
	At most 1	0.0002	3.5991	0.0578	3.5991	0.0578
MARUTI	None	0.0039	72.9507	0.0000	71.4472	0.0000
	At most 1	0.0001	1.5035	0.2201	1.5035	0.2201
NTPC	None	0.0027	52.3966	0.0000	48.2390	0.0000
	At most 1	0.0002	4.1575	0.0414	4.1575	0.0414
ONGC	None	0.0014	28.5794	0.0003	25.6839	0.0005
	At most 1	0.0002	2.8955	0.0888	2.8955	0.0888
PNB	None	0.0011	23.3282	0.0027	19.3794	0.0071
	At most 1	0.0002	3.9488	0.0469	3.9488	0.0469
POWERGRID	None	0.0038	74.2221	0.0000	67.4577	0.0000
	At most 1	0.0004	6.7644	0.0093	6.7644	0.0093
RANBAXY	None	0.0041	75.0819	0.0000	75.0039	0.0000
	At most 1	0.0000	0.0780	0.7800	0.0780	0.7800
RCOM	None	0.0056	101.4741	0.0001	101.3519	0.0000
	At most 1	0.0000	0.1222	0.7266	0.1222	0.7266
RELIANCE	None	0.0023	46.5107	0.0000	41.0073	0.0000
	At most 1	0.0003	5.5033	0.0190	5.5033	0.0190
RELINFRA	None	0.0024	43.4224	0.0000	42.8699	0.0000
	At most 1	0.0000	0.5525	0.4573	0.5525	0.4573
RPOWER	None	0.0037	67.8676	0.0000	67.2310	0.0000
	At most 1	0.0000	0.6367	0.4249	0.6367	0.4249
SAIL	None	0.0031	55.8108	0.0000	55.8100	0.0000
	At most 1	0.0000	0.0008	0.9780	0.0008	0.9780
SBIN	None	0.0015	30.6906	0.0001	27.6797	0.0002
	At most 1	0.0002	3.0109	0.0827	3.0109	0.0827
SESAGOA	None	0.0017	33.8175	0.0000	30.6436	0.0001
	At most 1	0.0002	3.1739	0.0748	3.1739	0.0748
SIEMENS	None	0.0080	132.9019	0.0001	131.3153	0.0001
	At most 1	0.0001	1.5866	0.2078	1.5866	0.2078
STER	None	0.0025	50.3614	0.0000	46.3948	0.0000

	At most 1	0.0002	3.9666	0.0464	3.9666	0.0464
SUNPHARMA	None	0.0046	83.2396	0.0000	83.2386	0.0000
	At most 1	0.0000	0.0011	0.9733	0.0011	0.9733
TATAMOTORS	None	0.0019	36.1036	0.0000	34.0242	0.0000
	At most 1	0.0001	2.0793	0.1493	2.0793	0.1493
TATAPOWER	None	0.0029	56.3548	0.0000	51.6220	0.0000
	At most 1	0.0003	4.7329	0.0296	4.7329	0.0296
TATASTEEL	None	0.0012	22.5798	0.0036	22.5402	0.0020
	At most 1	0.0000	0.0396	0.8423	0.0396	0.8423
TCS	None	0.0029	54.6499	0.0000	53.2289	0.0000
	At most 1	0.0001	1.4210	0.2332	1.4210	0.2332
WIPRO	None	0.0025	48.0755	0.0000	46.1393	0.0000
	At most 1	0.0001	1.9362	0.1641	1.9362	0.1641

Table 4A.3: Estimates of VECM for Individual Stocks-

	ACC		AMBUJACEM	
	Spot	Futures	Spot	Futures
Z (t−1)	0.0013	-0.0053*	-0.0042	-0.0102**
ΔS (t−1)	-0.2021**	0.3001**	-0.1663**	0.2774**
ΔS (t−2)	-0.0966**	0.1779**	-0.0646**	0.1339**
ΔS (t−3)	-0.0406**	0.121**	-0.0585**	0.0583**
ΔS (t−4)	-0.0095	0.0858**	-0.0193	0.0474**
ΔS (t−5)	0.0101	0.0435**	-0.0222	0.0118
ΔS (t−6)	NA	NA	NA	NA
ΔF (t−1)	0.1809**	-0.3183**	0.186**	-0.276**
ΔF (t−2)	0.0828**	-0.1959**	0.0929**	-0.1331**
ΔF (t−3)	0.04**	-0.129**	0.0437**	-0.0834**
ΔF (t−4)	0.0066	-0.0967**	0.0176	-0.049**
ΔF (t−5)	-0.0103	-0.0532**	0.0072	-0.0223
ΔF (t−6)	NA	NA	NA	NA
C	0.0001	0.002	0.0017	0.0032**

[Notes: ** and * denotes significance at 5% an 10% level respectively]

	AXISBANK		BAJAJAUTO	
	Spot	Futures	Spot	Futures
Z (t−1)	-0.0046**	-0.0061**	-0.0024	-0.0095**
ΔS (t−1)	-0.1421**	0.2665**	-0.2001**	0.2826**
ΔS (t−2)	-0.0769**	0.1169**	-0.0845**	0.1512**
ΔS (t−3)	-0.0252	0.0636**	-0.0257	0.1091**
ΔS (t−4)	-0.0164	0.0346	-0.018	0.0456**
ΔS (t−5)	NA	NA	NA	NA
ΔS (t−6)	NA	NA	NA	NA
ΔF (t−1)	0.1083**	-0.2928**	0.1535**	-0.3158**
ΔF (t−2)	0.0793**	-0.1137**	0.0808**	-0.153**
ΔF (t−3)	0.0308	-0.0574**	0.0324*	-0.1013**
ΔF (t−4)	0.0207	-0.0289	0.0077	-0.0548**
ΔF (t−5)	NA	NA	NA	NA
ΔF (t−6)	NA	NA	NA	NA
C	0.0014	0.0031**	-0.001	0.0031**

[Notes: ** and * denotes significance at 5% an 10% level respectively]

	BHARTIARTL		BHEL	
	Spot	Futures	Spot	Futures
Z (t−1)	-0.006	-0.0197**	0.0122**	0.0043
ΔS (t−1)	-0.1076**	0.3922**	-0.1346**	0.2589**
ΔS (t−2)	0.0388	0.3019**	-0.0123	0.1349**
ΔS (t−3)	0.0877**	0.2338**	NA	NA
ΔS (t−4)	0.0604**	0.136**	NA	NA
ΔS (t−5)	0.049*	0.0918**	NA	NA
ΔS (t−6)	NA	NA	NA	NA
ΔF (t−1)	0.0525**	-0.449**	0.1177**	-0.2664**
ΔF (t−2)	-0.0411	-0.3044**	0.0182	-0.1267**
ΔF (t−3)	-0.0974**	-0.2464**	NA	NA
ΔF (t−4)	-0.0581**	-0.1363**	NA	NA
ΔF (t−5)	-0.044*	-0.085**	NA	NA
ΔF (t−6)	NA	NA	NA	NA
C	0	0.0052**	-0.0035**	-0.0008

[Notes: ** and * denotes significance at 5% an 10% level respectively]

	BPCL		CAIRN	
	Spot	Futures	Spot	Futures
Z (t−1)	0	-0.0132**	0.0025	-0.0061**
ΔS (t−1)	-0.1618**	0.3823**	-0.0791**	0.3024**
ΔS (t−2)	-0.0914**	0.2359**	-0.0457**	0.1174**
ΔS (t−3)	-0.0426**	0.1607**	-0.0583**	-0.0047
ΔS (t−4)	-0.0214	0.1025**	-0.0474**	-0.0174
ΔS (t−5)	-0.0014	0.0546**	NA	NA
ΔS (t−6)	NA	NA	NA	NA
ΔF (t−1)	0.1575**	-0.3838**	0.0488**	-0.3379**
ΔF (t−2)	0.0998**	-0.2299**	0.0541**	-0.1211**
ΔF (t−3)	0.0642**	-0.1429**	0.0661**	0.0024
ΔF (t−4)	0.0238	-0.1058**	0.0617**	0.0205
ΔF (t−5)	-0.0002	-0.0606**	NA	NA
ΔF (t−6)	NA	NA	NA	NA
C	-0.0024	0.003	-0.0042**	-0.0011

[Notes: ** and * denotes significance at 5% an 10% level respectively]

	BPCL		CAIRN	
	Spot	Futures	Spot	Futures
Z (t−1)	0	-0.0132**	0.0025	-0.0061**
ΔS (t−1)	-0.1618**	0.3823**	-0.0791**	0.3024**
ΔS (t−2)	-0.0914**	0.2359**	-0.0457**	0.1174**
ΔS (t−3)	-0.0426**	0.1607**	-0.0583**	-0.0047
ΔS (t−4)	-0.0214	0.1025**	-0.0474**	-0.0174
ΔS (t−5)	-0.0014	0.0546**	NA	NA
ΔS (t−6)	NA	NA	NA	NA
ΔF (t−1)	0.1575**	-0.3838**	0.0488**	-0.3379**
ΔF (t−2)	0.0998**	-0.2299**	0.0541**	-0.1211**
ΔF (t−3)	0.0642**	-0.1429**	0.0661**	0.0024
ΔF (t−4)	0.0238	-0.1058**	0.0617**	0.0205
ΔF (t−5)	-0.0002	-0.0606**	NA	NA
ΔF (t−6)	NA	NA	NA	NA
C	-0.0024	0.003	-0.0042**	-0.0011

[Notes: ** and * denotes significance at 5% an 10% level respectively]

	CIPLA		COALINDIA	
	Spot	Futures	Spot	Futures
Z (t−1)	0.0019	-0.0125**	-0.0006	-0.003*
ΔS (t−1)	-0.1866**	0.3617**	-0.1447**	0.3596**
ΔS (t−2)	-0.0919**	0.2261**	-0.1086**	0.1683**
ΔS (t−3)	-0.0467**	0.1408**	-0.0362**	0.1097**
ΔS (t−4)	-0.0066	0.1067**	-0.0174	0.0425**
ΔS (t−5)	0.0119	0.0771**	NA	NA
ΔS (t−6)	NA	NA	NA	NA
ΔF (t−1)	0.1757**	-0.3704**	0.1195**	-0.3817**
ΔF (t−2)	0.0974**	-0.2234**	0.0885**	-0.1814**
ΔF (t−3)	0.0266	-0.1652**	0.049**	-0.0977**
ΔF (t−4)	-0.0113	-0.1251**	-0.0051	-0.0595**
ΔF (t−5)	-0.0145	-0.0754**	NA	NA
ΔF (t−6)	NA	NA	NA	NA
C	-0.0039*	0.0034*	-0.0018	-0.0004

[Notes: ** and * denotes significance at 5% an 10% level respectively]

	CIPLA		COALINDIA	
	Spot	Futures	Spot	Futures
Z (t−1)	0.0019	-0.0125**	-0.0006	-0.003*
ΔS (t−1)	-0.1866**	0.3617**	-0.1447**	0.3596**
ΔS (t−2)	-0.0919**	0.2261**	-0.1086**	0.1683**
ΔS (t−3)	-0.0467**	0.1408**	-0.0362**	0.1097**
ΔS (t−4)	-0.0066	0.1067**	-0.0174	0.0425**
ΔS (t−5)	0.0119	0.0771**	NA	NA
ΔS (t−6)	NA	NA	NA	NA
ΔF (t−1)	0.1757**	-0.3704**	0.1195**	-0.3817**
ΔF (t−2)	0.0974**	-0.2234**	0.0885**	-0.1814**
ΔF (t−3)	0.0266	-0.1652**	0.049**	-0.0977**
ΔF (t−4)	-0.0113	-0.1251**	-0.0051	-0.0595**
ΔF (t−5)	-0.0145	-0.0754**	NA	NA
ΔF (t−6)	NA	NA	NA	NA
C	-0.0039*	0.0034*	-0.0018	-0.0004

[Notes: ** and * denotes significance at 5% an 10% level respectively]

	DLF		DRREDDY	
	Spot	Futures	Spot	Futures
Z (t−1)	-0.0087*	-0.013**	0.0016	-0.0077**
ΔS (t−1)	-0.1972**	0.2443**	-0.1723**	0.3459**
ΔS (t−2)	-0.0764**	0.1361**	-0.0268	0.2533**
ΔS (t−3)	-0.029	0.0917**	-0.0346*	0.1332**
ΔS (t−4)	0.0156	0.0605*	-0.0115	0.0999**
ΔS (t−5)	0.0147	0.0304	-0.0053	0.0687**
ΔS (t−6)	NA	NA	0.0056	0.0439**
ΔF (t−1)	0.1789**	-0.2525**	0.1265**	-0.3766**
ΔF (t−2)	0.0879**	-0.1223**	0.0359**	-0.2457**
ΔF (t−3)	0.0341	-0.0868**	0.0148	-0.1632**
ΔF (t−4)	-0.0042	-0.0516	0.0088	-0.107**
ΔF (t−5)	-0.0044	-0.0244	0.0115	-0.0649**
ΔF (t−6)	NA	NA	-0.0122	-0.0526**
C	-0.0009	0.0019	-0.0013	0.0023

[Notes: ** and * denotes significance at 5% an 10% level respectively]

	GAIL		GRASIM	
	Spot	Futures	Spot	Futures
Z (t−1)	-0.0019	-0.0146**	0.0005	-0.0187**
ΔS (t−1)	-0.138**	0.4081**	-0.2519**	0.3287**
ΔS (t−2)	-0.0971**	0.2263**	-0.1838**	0.1772**
ΔS (t−3)	-0.0381**	0.1559**	-0.1267**	0.1043**
ΔS (t−4)	-0.023	0.0854**	-0.0872**	0.0659**
ΔS (t−5)	-0.0135	0.0667**	-0.0409**	0.0344**
ΔS (t−6)	0.0172	0.0578**	-0.034**	0.0067
ΔF (t−1)	0.1157**	-0.4184**	0.2341**	-0.3156**
ΔF (t−2)	0.0573**	-0.2602**	0.1778**	-0.1697**
ΔF (t−3)	0.0512**	-0.1412**	0.1277**	-0.0924**
ΔF (t−4)	0.014	-0.0986**	0.1007**	-0.06**
ΔF (t−5)	0.0019	-0.0736**	0.0635**	-0.0266*
ΔF (t−6)	-0.0127	-0.0558**	0.04**	-0.0105
C	-0.0031**	0.0014	-0.0002	0.0074**

[Notes: ** and * denotes significance at 5% an 10% level respectively]

	HCLTECH		HDFC	
	Spot	Futures	Spot	Futures
Z (t−1)	0.0029	-0.011**	0.0026	-0.0011
ΔS (t−1)	-0.1134**	0.3677**	-0.1703**	0.2339**
ΔS (t−2)	-0.0279	0.2139**	-0.0733**	0.1148**
ΔS (t−3)	0.024	0.1382**	-0.0193	0.0443**
ΔS (t−4)	0.0188	0.0893**	-0.0077	0.0351*
ΔS (t−5)	0.027	0.0531**	NA	NA
ΔS (t−6)	NA	NA	NA	NA
ΔF (t−1)	0.0813**	-0.4063**	0.1556**	-0.2691**
ΔF (t−2)	0.0317	-0.2237**	0.0836**	-0.1147**
ΔF (t−3)	-0.0296	-0.1578**	0.0354	-0.0353*
ΔF (t−4)	-0.0078	-0.0863**	0.0058	-0.0383**
ΔF (t−5)	-0.0266	-0.0536**	NA	NA
ΔF (t−6)	NA	NA	NA	NA
C	-0.0017	0.0032**	-0.0005	0.0006

[Notes: ** and * denotes significance at 5% an 10% level respectively]

	HDFCBANK		HEROMOTOCO	
	Spot	Futures	Spot	Futures
Z (t−1)	-0.0004	-0.0069**	-0.0007	-0.004**
ΔS (t−1)	-0.1973**	0.195**	-0.1719**	0.2509**
ΔS (t−2)	-0.0702**	0.1057**	-0.0633**	0.1193**
ΔS (t−3)	-0.0464**	0.0442**	-0.0528**	0.0344*
ΔS (t−4)	-0.05**	0.0016	-0.0349**	0.0091
ΔS (t−5)	-0.0166	0.0237	NA	NA
ΔS (t−6)	NA	NA	NA	NA
ΔF (t−1)	0.1522**	-0.259**	0.1565**	-0.2455**
ΔF (t−2)	0.0723**	-0.1106**	0.0721**	-0.1053**
ΔF (t−3)	0.0408*	-0.0557**	0.0418**	-0.0496**
ΔF (t−4)	0.0404*	-0.0072	0.0136	-0.0239
ΔF (t−5)	0.0124	-0.0203	NA	NA
ΔF (t−6)	NA	NA	NA	NA
C	0.0019	0.0045**	-0.0009	0.0001

[Notes: ** and * denotes significance at 5% an 10% level respectively]

	HINDALCO		HINDUNILVR	
	Spot	Futures	Spot	Futures
Z (t−1)	0.0031	-0.0114*	0.0046	-0.0008
ΔS (t−1)	-0.2547**	0.301**	-0.1813**	0.2476**
ΔS (t−2)	-0.1039**	0.2159**	-0.0058	0.1681**
ΔS (t−3)	-0.1017**	0.0867**	0.0063	0.092**
ΔS (t−4)	-0.0247	0.0968**	-0.0024	0.0375**
ΔS (t−5)	-0.0016	0.052**	NA	NA
ΔS (t−6)	NA	NA	NA	NA
ΔF (t−1)	0.2367**	-0.3129**	0.2006**	-0.2381**
ΔF (t−2)	0.1043**	-0.2131**	0.0268	-0.1542**
ΔF (t−3)	0.1023**	-0.0861**	-0.0197	-0.1113**
ΔF (t−4)	0.0299	-0.0924**	0.0176	-0.0291
ΔF (t−5)	0.0181	-0.0382	NA	NA
ΔF (t−6)	NA	NA	NA	NA
C	-0.004	0.0025	-0.0011	0.0011

[Notes: ** and * denotes significance at 5% an 10% level respectively]

	ICICIBANK		IDFC	
	Spot	Futures	Spot	Futures
Z (t−1)	-0.0031	-0.0042*	-0.0033	-0.0048*
ΔS (t−1)	-0.2072**	0.1886**	-0.1673**	0.3422**
ΔS (t−2)	-0.1032**	0.0741**	-0.0829**	0.2072**
ΔS (t−3)	-0.0996**	-0.0109	-0.0625**	0.1141**
ΔS (t−4)	NA	NA	-0.0744**	0.0176
ΔS (t−5)	NA	NA	-0.0559**	-0.0048
ΔS (t−6)	NA	NA	NA	NA
ΔF (t−1)	0.1734**	-0.2212**	0.1557**	-0.3563**
ΔF (t−2)	0.0983**	-0.087**	0.0929**	-0.202**
ΔF (t−3)	0.1016**	0.007	0.0655**	-0.1079**
ΔF (t−4)	NA	NA	0.0905**	-0.0081
ΔF (t−5)	NA	NA	0.0553**	0.0022
ΔF (t−6)	NA	NA	NA	NA
C	-0.0005	0.0005	-0.0005	0.001

[Notes: ** and * denotes significance at 5% an 10% level respectively]

	INFY		ITC	
	Spot	Futures	Spot	Futures
Z (t−1)	0.0005	-0.0028	-0.0054**	-0.009**
ΔS (t−1)	-0.1713**	0.2509**	-0.2315**	0.2318**
ΔS (t−2)	-0.0362	0.1533**	-0.134**	0.098**
ΔS (t−3)	-0.0036	0.0682**	-0.0363*	0.0566**
ΔS (t−4)	NA	NA	NA	NA
ΔS (t−5)	NA	NA	NA	NA
ΔS (t−6)	NA	NA	NA	NA
ΔF (t−1)	0.1473**	-0.278**	0.1993**	-0.2713**
ΔF (t−2)	0.0207	-0.17**	0.1411**	-0.0925**
ΔF (t−3)	-0.0016	-0.0761**	0.0405**	-0.0603**
ΔF (t−4)	NA	NA	NA	NA
ΔF (t−5)	NA	NA	NA	NA
ΔF (t−6)	NA	NA	NA	NA
C	-0.0005	0.0011	0.0034**	0.0054**

[Notes: ** and * denotes significance at 5% an 10% level respectively]

	JINDALSTEL		JPASSOCIAT	
	Spot	Futures	Spot	Futures
Z (t−1)	0.0118	-0.0071	-0.004	-0.0086**
ΔS (t−1)	-0.1777**	0.2675**	-0.2484**	0.2415**
ΔS (t−2)	-0.1355**	0.0907**	-0.1161**	0.1176**
ΔS (t−3)	-0.1073**	0.0265	-0.0662**	0.0349
ΔS (t−4)	-0.0406	0.0406	0.0128	0.0585**
ΔS (t−5)	-0.0352	0.0208	NA	NA
ΔS (t−6)	0.0126	0.0304	NA	NA
ΔF (t−1)	0.1677**	-0.2921**	0.2376**	-0.2438**
ΔF (t−2)	0.1365**	-0.1052**	0.1456**	-0.0863**
ΔF (t−3)	0.1081**	-0.0268	0.0666**	-0.034
ΔF (t−4)	0.0464*	-0.0347	-0.0073	-0.0539**
ΔF (t−5)	0.0333	-0.0203	NA	NA
ΔF (t−6)	0.0035	-0.0123	NA	NA
C	-0.0098**	-0.0027	-0.0022	0.0003

[Notes: ** and * denotes significance at 5% an 10% level respectively]

	KOTAKBANK		LT	
	Spot	Futures	Spot	Futures
Z (t−1)	-0.0045	-0.025**	-0.0081**	-0.0122**
ΔS (t−1)	-0.2615**	0.2145**	-0.1416**	0.3177**
ΔS (t−2)	-0.1433**	0.1135**	-0.0826**	0.1477**
ΔS (t−3)	-0.1108**	0.0377**	-0.0624**	0.0406
ΔS (t−4)	-0.0819**	0.0111	NA	NA
ΔS (t−5)	-0.0175	0.0301*	NA	NA
ΔS (t−6)	-0.0085	0.0242	NA	NA
ΔF (t−1)	0.2109**	-0.2746**	0.1235**	-0.3363**
ΔF (t−2)	0.1152**	-0.1441**	0.1014**	-0.1317**
ΔF (t−3)	0.1082**	-0.0484**	0.0626**	-0.0382
ΔF (t−4)	0.0854**	-0.0152	NA	NA
ΔF (t−5)	0.0376**	-0.0161	NA	NA
ΔF (t−6)	0.0212	-0.004	NA	NA
C	0.0025	0.0106**	0.0018	0.0035**

[Notes: ** and * denotes significance at 5% an 10% level respectively]

	M&M		MARUTI	
	Spot	Futures	Spot	Futures
Z (t−1)	-0.0017	-0.0087**	-0.0024	-0.0117**
ΔS (t−1)	-0.2096**	0.2773**	-0.1367**	0.3142**
ΔS (t−2)	-0.0916**	0.1802**	-0.0459**	0.1666**
ΔS (t−3)	-0.0515**	0.1064**	-0.0274	0.0705**
ΔS (t−4)	0.0032	0.075**	-0.0032	0.0541**
ΔS (t−5)	NA	NA	-0.0138	0.0208
ΔS (t−6)	NA	NA	NA	NA
ΔF (t−1)	0.1731**	-0.3195**	0.1369**	-0.3175**
ΔF (t−2)	0.0858**	-0.1859**	0.0513**	-0.1692**
ΔF (t−3)	0.0678**	-0.0936**	0.0094	-0.0945**
ΔF (t−4)	0.008	-0.0651**	-0.0046	-0.0655**
ΔF (t−5)	NA	NA	0.0168	-0.0176
ΔF (t−6)	NA	NA	NA	NA
C	0.0017	0.0044**	0.0007	0.0043**

[Notes: ** and * denotes significance at 5% an 10% level respectively]

	NTPC		ONGC	
	Spot	Futures	Spot	Futures
Z (t−1)	0.0022	-0.0066**	0.0014	-0.0027
ΔS (t−1)	-0.1451**	0.4025**	-0.1322**	0.3627**
ΔS (t−2)	-0.079**	0.2126**	-0.0892**	0.1907**
ΔS (t−3)	-0.0319*	0.1105**	-0.0385*	0.1102**
ΔS (t−4)	-0.0252	0.0519**	0.0229	0.0895**
ΔS (t−5)	-0.0348**	0.0112	NA	NA
ΔS (t−6)	NA	NA	NA	NA
ΔF (t−1)	0.1336**	-0.4137**	0.1202**	-0.3796**
ΔF (t−2)	0.0742**	-0.2274**	0.1132**	-0.1671**
ΔF (t−3)	0.0321*	-0.1167**	0.048**	-0.1026**
ΔF (t−4)	0.0123	-0.062**	-0.021	-0.0872**
ΔF (t−5)	0.0274*	-0.0216	NA	NA
ΔF (t−6)	NA	NA	NA	NA
C	-0.0021*	0.0007	-0.002	-0.0006

[Notes: ** and * denotes significance at 5% an 10% level respectively]

	PNB		POWERGRID	
	Spot	Futures	Spot	Futures
Z (t−1)	-0.0017	-0.0036	0.008**	-0.0045
ΔS (t−1)	-0.2205**	0.2855**	-0.1571**	0.3891**
ΔS (t−2)	-0.1017**	0.1633**	-0.0821**	0.2333**
ΔS (t−3)	-0.0606**	0.0737**	-0.0552**	0.1312**
ΔS (t−4)	-0.0289	0.0348	-0.0365**	0.0837**
ΔS (t−5)	NA	NA	-0.0237	0.0317**
ΔS (t−6)	NA	NA	NA	NA
ΔF (t−1)	0.2168**	-0.2731**	0.1419**	-0.4113**
ΔF (t−2)	0.1156**	-0.1476**	0.0748**	-0.2487**
ΔF (t−3)	0.0695**	-0.0644**	0.06**	-0.1373**
ΔF (t−4)	0.0496**	-0.0163	0.0343**	-0.0925**
ΔF (t−5)	NA	NA	0.0248	-0.0282*
ΔF (t−6)	NA	NA	NA	NA
C	-0.0011	0.0001	-0.0035**	0.0012

[Notes: ** and * denotes significance at 5% an 10% level respectively]

	RANBAXY		RCOM	
	Spot	Futures	Spot	Futures
Z (t−1)	0.0063	-0.0087	0.013	-0.0091
ΔS (t−1)	-0.2388**	0.2979**	-0.2798**	0.3024**
ΔS (t−2)	-0.1422**	0.1666**	-0.159**	0.1851**
ΔS (t−3)	-0.0949**	0.088**	-0.1129**	0.0963**
ΔS (t−4)	-0.0402*	0.0864**	-0.0241	0.1129**
ΔS (t−5)	0.0196	0.1132**	-0.0748**	0.0042
ΔS (t−6)	-0.0349*	0.0103	-0.0249	0.016
ΔF (t−1)	0.2237**	-0.3034**	0.2716**	-0.2961**
ΔF (t−2)	0.1327**	-0.1745**	0.1862**	-0.1515**
ΔF (t−3)	0.0919**	-0.0943**	0.1129**	-0.0969**
ΔF (t−4)	0.0395*	-0.0838**	0.0382	-0.0953**
ΔF (t−5)	-0.0184	-0.1082**	0.084**	0.0083
ΔF (t−6)	0.0493**	0.0038	0.0366	-0.001
C	-0.0061**	0.0009	-0.0061	0.0028

[Notes: ** and * denotes significance at 5% an 10% level respectively]

	RELIANCE		RELINFRA	
	Spot	Futures	Spot	Futures
Z (t−1)	0.0005	-0.0034	0.0051	-0.0011
ΔS (t−1)	-0.1791**	0.2537**	-0.2503**	0.2805**
ΔS (t−2)	-0.0979**	0.1292**	-0.1616**	0.1344**
ΔS (t−3)	0.0091	0.1223**	-0.0785**	0.0929**
ΔS (t−4)	-0.0266	0.0317	-0.0519	0.0431
ΔS (t−5)	NA	NA	-0.0005	0.0495
ΔS (t−6)	NA	NA	NA	NA
ΔF (t−1)	0.1448**	-0.2911**	0.2266**	-0.2831**
ΔF (t−2)	0.0917**	-0.1315**	0.1778**	-0.1042**
ΔF (t−3)	-0.0001	-0.1186**	0.0961**	-0.0707**
ΔF (t−4)	0.0225	-0.0347	0.0545*	-0.0412
ΔF (t−5)	NA	NA	0.0205	-0.0337
ΔF (t−6)	NA	NA	NA	NA
C	-0.0023	-0.0005	-0.0057**	-0.0029

[Notes: ** and * denotes significance at 5% an 10% level respectively]

	RPOWER		SAIL	
	Spot	Futures	Spot	Futures
Z (t−1)	0.0028	-0.009	0.0079**	0.0009
ΔS (t−1)	-0.3218**	0.2801**	-0.2508**	0.3602**
ΔS (t−2)	-0.2422**	0.1257**	-0.1639**	0.2028**
ΔS (t−3)	-0.0978**	0.1362**	-0.1189**	0.119**
ΔS (t−4)	-0.0815**	0.0698**	-0.0774**	0.0862**
ΔS (t−5)	-0.0263	0.065**	-0.0561**	0.054**
ΔS (t−6)	-0.012	0.0239	-0.0372**	0.0117
ΔF (t−1)	0.2863**	-0.2862**	0.224**	-0.3623**
ΔF (t−2)	0.2362**	-0.1178**	0.1753**	-0.1908**
ΔF (t−3)	0.1185**	-0.1117**	0.1262**	-0.1165**
ΔF (t−4)	0.0859**	-0.0596**	0.0716**	-0.0946**
ΔF (t−5)	0.0292	-0.0584**	0.0509**	-0.0593**
ΔF (t−6)	0.0242	-0.0107	0.0422**	-0.0087
C	-0.0071**	-0.0008	-0.0074**	-0.0047**

[Notes: ** and * denotes significance at 5% an 10% level respectively]

	SBIN		SESAGOA	
	Spot	Futures	Spot	Futures
Z (t−1)	0.0017	-0.0005	0.0029	-0.0022
ΔS (t−1)	-0.181**	0.1832**	-0.2272**	0.249**
ΔS (t−2)	-0.0727**	0.0596*	-0.1132**	0.1361**
ΔS (t−3)	0.0168	0.06**	-0.0985**	0.0275
ΔS (t−4)	NA	NA	-0.0501**	0.0209
ΔS (t−5)	NA	NA	-0.0338*	0.0061
ΔS (t−6)	NA	NA	NA	NA
ΔF (t−1)	0.1442**	-0.2048**	0.1921**	-0.2653**
ΔF (t−2)	0.0626**	-0.0677**	0.1097**	-0.13**
ΔF (t−3)	0.0111	-0.036	0.1031**	-0.028
ΔF (t−4)	NA	NA	0.0485**	-0.0197
ΔF (t−5)	NA	NA	0.0274	-0.0096
ΔF (t−6)	NA	NA	NA	NA
C	-0.0029**	-0.0012	-0.0041**	-0.0018

[Notes: ** and * denotes significance at 5% an 10% level respectively]

	SIEMENS		STER	
	Spot	Futures	Spot	Futures
Z (t−1)	0.0181**	-0.0302**	0.0007	-0.0075*
ΔS (t−1)	-0.2043**	0.3678**	-0.2271**	0.3318**
ΔS (t−2)	-0.1205**	0.2212**	-0.1081**	0.2353**
ΔS (t−3)	-0.0762**	0.1283**	-0.0383	0.1636**
ΔS (t−4)	-0.0351**	0.088**	-0.0267	0.0861**
ΔS (t−5)	-0.046**	0.0202	-0.0109	0.0481**
ΔS (t−6)	-0.0275*	0.0085	NA	NA
ΔF (t−1)	0.2123**	-0.3359**	0.1976**	-0.3518**
ΔF (t−2)	0.131**	-0.2077**	0.1065**	-0.2321**
ΔF (t−3)	0.088**	-0.1302**	0.05**	-0.152**
ΔF (t−4)	0.0499**	-0.0726**	0.0276	-0.084**
ΔF (t−5)	0.0549**	-0.012	0.0139	-0.0451**
ΔF (t−6)	0.0276*	-0.0112	NA	NA
C	-0.0088**	0.0078**	-0.0026	-0.0007

[Notes: ** and * denotes significance at 5% an 10% level respectively]

	SUNPHARMA		TATAMOTORS	
	Spot	Futures	Spot	Futures
Z (t−1)	-0.0066	-0.0223**	0.0039	0.0003
ΔS (t−1)	-0.1668**	0.3817**	-0.1512**	0.293**
ΔS (t−2)	-0.0503**	0.2623**	0.0128	0.2261**
ΔS (t−3)	-0.0307	0.1475**	-0.001	0.0994**
ΔS (t−4)	0.0273	0.1328**	NA	NA
ΔS (t−5)	0.0037	0.0535**	NA	NA
ΔS (t−6)	NA	NA	NA	NA
ΔF (t−1)	0.1385**	-0.4064**	0.1146**	-0.3306**
ΔF (t−2)	0.0527**	-0.2695**	-0.0064	-0.2204**
ΔF (t−3)	0.0161	-0.1658**	-0.009	-0.1111**
ΔF (t−4)	-0.0188	-0.1311**	NA	NA
ΔF (t−5)	-0.0074	-0.0581**	NA	NA
ΔF (t−6)	NA	NA	NA	NA
C	0.003	0.0105**	-0.0015	0.0003

[Notes: ** and * denotes significance at 5% an 10% level respectively]

	TATAPOWER		TATASTEEL	
	Spot	Futures	Spot	Futures
Z (t−1)	-0.0001	-0.0117**	0	-0.0017
ΔS (t−1)	-0.2215**	0.3884**	-0.2303**	0.2172**
ΔS (t−2)	-0.1046**	0.2696**	-0.0508*	0.1614**
ΔS (t−3)	-0.0624**	0.1561**	-0.0127	0.079**
ΔS (t−4)	-0.0176	0.1185**	NA	NA
ΔS (t−5)	-0.0125	0.0668**	NA	NA
ΔS (t−6)	NA	NA	NA	NA
ΔF (t−1)	0.1733**	-0.414**	0.1951**	-0.2345**
ΔF (t−2)	0.1036**	-0.2622**	0.0474*	-0.1588**
ΔF (t−3)	0.062**	-0.1593**	0.0273	-0.0633**
ΔF (t−4)	0.025	-0.1094**	NA	NA
ΔF (t−5)	0.0249*	-0.0547**	NA	NA
ΔF (t−6)	NA	NA	NA	NA
C	-0.0037**	0.0013	-0.0053**	-0.0041**

[Notes: ** and * denotes significance at 5% an 10% level respectively]

	TCS		WIPRO	
	Spot	Futures	Spot	Futures
Z (t−1)	-0.0023	-0.0084**	0.0002	-0.0078**
ΔS (t−1)	-0.1402**	0.2926**	-0.1468**	0.3747**
ΔS (t−2)	-0.038*	0.1619**	-0.0852**	0.22**
ΔS (t−3)	-0.0071	0.0847**	-0.0517**	0.1248**
ΔS (t−4)	0.0042	0.0502**	-0.0381*	0.0672**
ΔS (t−5)	NA	NA	-0.0464**	0.0308
ΔS (t−6)	NA	NA	-0.0052	0.0234
ΔF (t−1)	0.0896**	-0.3461**	0.1603**	-0.364**
ΔF (t−2)	0.0232	-0.1773**	0.0706**	-0.2296**
ΔF (t−3)	-0.0034	-0.1006**	0.0404**	-0.1433**
ΔF (t−4)	-0.018	-0.0602**	0.0312	-0.0767**
ΔF (t−5)	NA	NA	0.0526**	-0.0267
ΔF (t−6)	NA	NA	0.0008	-0.0324*
C	0.0008	0.003**	-0.0021	0.0004

[Notes: ** and * denotes significance at 5% an 10% level respectively]

Lightning Source UK Ltd.
Milton Keynes UK
UKHW010702160223
417122UK00019B/1656